# Interior Sketches II
## More Ramblings around Interior Alaska historic sites
### Text and drawings by Ray Bonnell

Pingo Press - Fairbanks, Alaska

Artwork, graphics and text copyright 2023 by Ray Bonnell.

All rights reserved. No part of this publication may be reproduced, stored in a retrieved system, or transmitted in any form or by any means—electronic, mechanical, photocopying, or otherwise—without the prior written permission of the publisher.

All drawings and essays related to specific historic sites were originally published in *Sketches of Alaska,* a biweekly column appearing in the *Fairbanks Daily News-Miner.* Some of the essays have been revised and expanded since original publication.

Book design, layout and formatting done at Pingo Press. Fonts used: Licinia Aged, Gil Sans, Minion Pro

Cover illustration: Nenana train depot (see page 52)

Frontispiece: View from inside John Haines' cabin at Richardson, looking out over the Tanana River Valley)

This book would not have been possible without the support of my wife, Betsy, who has been my companion for fifty years, and voluntarily (yes—voluntarily) edits my work and acts as an artistic consultant; and the willingness of my first editor at the *Fairbanks Daily News-Miner,* Glenn BurnSilver, to give me a chance to show what I could do.

127 Glacier Avenue. Fairbanks, AK 99701
info@pingopress.us

Printed in the United States of America
Second Edition, Revised and Updated, April 2023
ISBN 978-1-7364236-4-6

# Contents

Map ........................................................................................................................................... 1

Ode of the North ..................................................................................................................... 2

**Eagle City Hall reflects city's pioneer days** ............................................................................ 4
    Eagle, Taylor Highway

**Northern Commercial Company helped city of Eagle survive** ............................................. 6
    Eagle, Taylor Highway

**Roald Amundsen cabin in Eagle – a link with bygone era of Polar exploration** ................... 8
    Eagle, Taylor Highway

**Tisha's schoolhouse and old town of Chicken still attract visitors** ..................................... 10
    Chicken, Taylor Highway

**From Fairbanks to Chicken, a long road for FE Company's Dredge No. 4** ....................... 12
    Chicken, Taylor Highway

**The Fortymile Roadhouse – gateway to the historic Fortymile country** ........................... 14
    Tetlin Junction, Taylor Highway

**1942 CAA Truck and Northway Airfield - parts of Alaska aviation history** ....................... 16
    Northway Junction, Alaska Highway

**Sullivan Roadhouse finds rebuilt life in Delta Junction** ..................................................... 18
    Delta Junction, Richardson Highway

**Rika's Roadhouse still important fixture along Richardson Highway** ............................... 20
    Big Delta, Richardson Highway

**Alaska Road Commission's Big Delta ferry – of roads, truckers, and tolls** ....................... 22
    Big Delta, Richardson Highway

**Bingle Memorial Camp namesake was indefatigable worker** ............................................ 24
    Harding Lake, Richardson Highway

**Denali Highway history and Whitey's cabin at Maclaren River** ........................................ 26
    Maclaren River, Denali Highway

**Brushkana Creek cabin a remnant of Denali transportation history** ................................ 28
    Brushkana Creek, Denali Highway

**The East Fork cabin – Adolf Murie's base camp for pioneering wolf studies** ................... 30
    Toklat River East Fork, Denali National Park and Preserve

# Contents

**Kantishna's Fannie Quigley, a larger-than-life frontier woman**...............32
   Kantishna, Denali National Park and Preserve

**Emil Usibelli and the early years of Usibelli Coal Mine**...............34
   Healy, Parks Highway

**Nenana Native cemetery is a peaceful place to visit**...............36
   Nenana, Parks Highway

**Railroad dramatically changed Nenana**...............38
   Nenana, Parks Highway

**Manley Roadhouse – serving hospitality since 1903**...............40
   Manley, Elliott Highway

**Old Gilmore/McCarty Mill near Fairbanks may soon disappear**...............42
   Fairbanks Creek Road, Steese Highway

**Homestake Mine's Nordale Adit is a remnant of area's lode mining history**...............44
   Fairbanks Creek Road, Steese Highway

**Samppi Mine near Chatanika typical of old drift mines that dot Interior Alaska**...............46
   Chatanika, Steese Highway

**Mining remnants still visible in Nome Creek Basin**...............48
   Nome Creek, Steese Highway

**Remote Sourdough Creek camp offered modern conveniences in 1930s**...............50
   Sourdough Creek, Steese Highwayy

**Fairbanks-Circle Trail gradually morphed into Steese Highway**...............52
   Central, Steese Highway

**Venerable Central Roadhouse almost made it to 21st century**...............54
   Central, Steese Highway

**Ups and downs of Circle City, the "Paris of the North"**...............56
   Circle, Steese Highway

**Circle's Rasmussen House a freighting pioneer's legacy**...............58
   Circle, Steese Highwa

**Colorado Creek Roadhouse welcomed travellers headed to Chena Hot Springs**...............60
   Colorado Creek, Chena Hot Springs Road

**Independent Lumber warehouse a reminder of early lumbering history**...............62
   Downtown Fairbanks, Clay Street

# Contents

*Clay Street Cemetery helps preserve Fairbanks history* ........................................................................... **64**
    Downtown Fairbanks, Clay Street

*Main School, now City Hall, is a Fairbanks landmark* ............................................................................ **66**
    Downtown Fairbanks, Cushman Street

*Old Federal Building anchors downtown district* ..................................................................................... **68**
    Downtown Fairbanks, Cushman Street

*Gilcher Building displays city's last old-time storefront* ............................................................................ **70**
    Downtown Fairbanks, 3rd Avenue

*Empress Theater brought several firsts to Fairbanks* ................................................................................ **72**
    Downtown Fairbanks, 2nd Avenue

*Second Avenue cabin was a safe haven for Clara Rust in 1909* ............................................................. **74**
    Downtown Fairbanks, 2nd Avenue

*Blue Crystal Water Company delivered tasty water around early Fairbanks* ......................................... **76**
    Downtown Fairbanks, Cowles Street

*White Seal Dock a leftover from Fairbanks early waterfront* .................................................................. **78**
    Downtown Fairbanks, Cowles Street

*Mary Lee Davis House – from plush early Fairbanks home to modern B&B* ....................................... **80**
    Downtown Fairbanks, Cowles Street

*Patty House is a testament to city's comign of age* ................................................................................... **82**
    Downtown Fairbanks, 6th Avenue

*Claypool/Berry house a reminder of Fairbanks judicial history* ............................................................. **84**
    Downtown Fairbanks. 1st Avenue

*Life on the Line in Fairbanks historic red light district* .......................................................................... **86**
    Pioneer Park, Gold Rush Town

*Harding Car a part of Alaska presidential history* .................................................................................. **88**
    Pioneer Park, Gold Rush Town

*Big I Pub dispenses history as well as hospitality* ..................................................................................... **90**
    Fairbanks, Garden Island, N Cushman Street

*Street widening gives clearer view of historic Noyes House* .................................................................... **92**
    Fairbanks, Illinois Street

*Fairbanks Exploration Company machine shop kept dredges running* .................................................. **94**
    Fairbanks, Railroad Industrial Area, Charles Street

# Contents

*Slaterville: from hayfields to housig developments* ..................................................................96
    Fairbanks - Slaterville, Well Street

*Skiing at Birch Hill in Fairbanks dates back to the 1930s* ..........................................................98
    Fairbanks - Slaterville, Well Street

*Alaska's last territorial governor, Mike Stepovich, called Fairbanks home* ............................... 100
    Fairbanks - Slaterville, Charles Street

*Slaterville comes of age, complete with gas pumps* ................................................................. 102
    Fairbanks - Slaterville, Minnie Street

*Despite commercialization, homes can still be found in Graehl, Fairbanks' first suburb* ..................... 104
    Fairbanks - Graehl, Front Street

*The early Richardson Highway and the Gibson Stage Line* ..................................................... 106
    Fairbanks, College Road, Fountainhead Antique Auto Museum

*Lemeta is an eclectic mix of rustic cabins and modern homes* ................................................. 108
    Fairbanks, Lemeta, O'Connor Road

*The early years of Creamer's Dairy* ........................................................................................... 110
    Fairbanks, College Road, Creamers Field

*Tanana Valley State Fair a long-time tradition in Fairbanks* ..................................................... 112
    Fairbanks, College Road, Tanana Valley State Fairgrounds

*Birch Hill Cemetery established to honor's a wife's final wish* .................................................. 114
    Fairbanks, Birch Hill

*KFAR Radio – Cap Lathrop's gift to Interior Alaska* ................................................................. 116
    Fairbanks, Farmers Loop

*UAF Experiment Farm history reflects saga of Alaska agriculture* ........................................... 118
    Fairbanks. University of Alaska, W. Tanana Drive

*Constitution Hall played important role in state's formation* .................................................. 120
    Fairbanks, University of Alaska, Tok Lane

*Bunnell House still an important part of university* ................................................................. 122
    Fairbanks, University of Alaska, Chatanika Drive

*Fairbanks Exploration Company's pump house a watering hole of a different sort* ..................... 124
    Fairbanks, Chena Pump Road

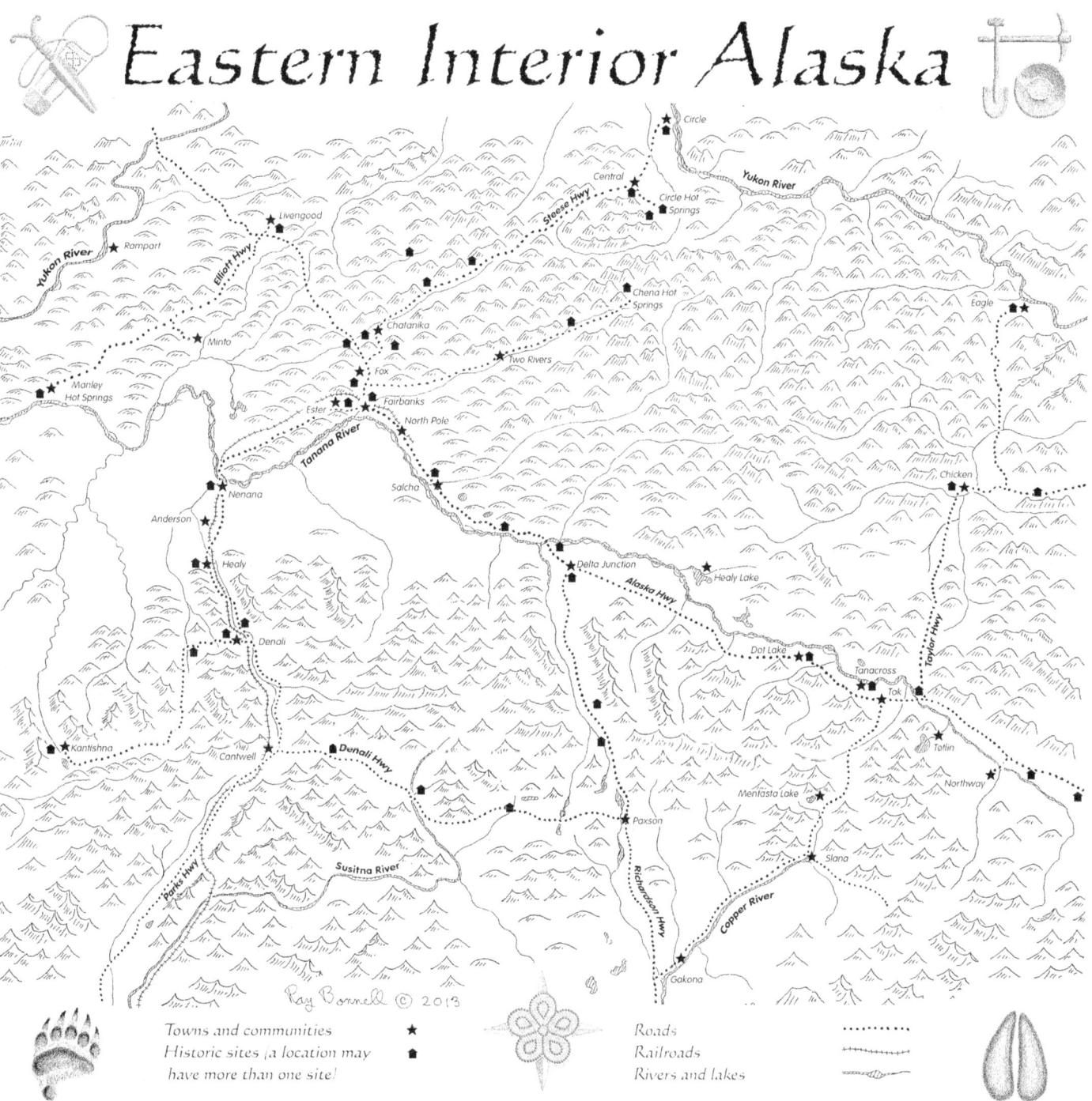

Ode of the North

# Ode of the North

by Joseph Ulmer (found tacked to the wall of a cabin on Deadwood Creek)

*Take a drink with a friend or friends when you have a chance.*

*When using a man's cabin and before leaving wash the dishes, leave shavings and kindling and as much wood cut as you used. Also, close the door of the cabin. If barricaded against bears, put the barricade back.*

*Never ask a man what religion he has for the great outdoors is his place of worship.*

*Never speak of women disrespectfully; we all had mothers.*

*Always give a fellow a lift if the going is tough.*

*Don't abuse a dog. He is the best friend you have on the trail. Be kind to dumb animals, they remember you.*

*Don't kill any game wantonly…only what you have to kill for your need or for someone who is out of meat.*

*Call the musher in and offer him a mug up or feed and if he is tired give him a shakedown.*

*Don't waste any animal by shooting at them for targets. The last cartridge may save your life.*

*Keep your matches and footgear dry on the trail and never drink whisky or other spirits on the trail; it may be fatal to you.*

*Don't wander around when the fog comes in and you can't see where you are going; wait till it clears up.*

*Don't leave any lights or candles burning or heavy fire in the stove when you are away from the cabin.*

*Don't set fire to the woods. It will destroy the wildlife and game.*

*Parboil your bacon before frying; it will not cause you so much rheumatism. Also, be sanitary about the camp so as not to pollute the water and atmosphere.*

*Don't tell the other fellow your troubles, especially love or matrimonial affairs. He may have a lot of his own.*

*Keep off the other fellow's trapline, both literally and categorically speaking.*

Joseph Ulmer (1874-1958) prospected around Interior Alaska before settling in the Circle Hot Springs area. In addition to mining, he worked as an engineer for the Alaska Road Commission and was a Territorial Road Commissioner. He was an inveterate writer—penning scientific and historical articles, satire, criticism and poetry. Ulmer published newspaper columns under the pen name, "Cassiar Joe."

Taylor Highway - Eagle

Eagle City Hall in 1999

## Eagle City Hall reflects city's pioneer days

The City of Eagle sits beside the Yukon River six miles west of the Canadian border. It was established by disappointed miners returning from the Klondike, but mining is only part of the area's history.

Eagle is located along the Yukon's west bank, south of Mission Creek. In 1874 a French-Canadian fur trader, Moses Mercier, started a trading post called Belle Island about three miles to the north near a Han Athabascan village.

A few years later he moved the trading post to the mouth of Mission Creek. Han called the creek Tototlindu, but an Episcopal mission (only lasting a few years) next to Mercier's trading post led to the creek's renaming. The trading post itself only operated intermittently.

Han have occupied the Upper Yukon region from Charley River (55 miles downriver from Eagle) to the Klondike River (60 miles upriver at Dawson City) for generations. (Eagle Native village is still located just upriver from Eagle.) Archaeological excavations at the Eagle courthouse in 1975 uncovered evidence of Native occupation hundreds of years prior to Western contact.

Gold had been found in Alaska's Upper Yukon region many years before the 1897 Klondike Gold Rush. A strike was made along the Fortymile River in 1886, and in 1895 gold was discovered on American Creek (a tributary of Mission Creek). However, when the fabulous strikes along the Klondike River were publicized, most of these miners left Alaska for the Yukon.

A few popular histories place Eagle's beginning in 1897. While some miners may have camped at Mission Creek in 1897, period documents indicate the town actually began coalescing in 1898.

U.S. Army Captain P.H. Ray, who travelled to Alaska in 1897 to investigate rumors of civil unrest and scout out locations for Army posts, traveled up the Yukon River as far as Canada's border in Fall 1897. In an Oct. 6 letter he described the Mission Creek area as an excellent location for a military post, but did not mention any settlement there. He also recommended that posts be established away from mining towns so that "troops, if required to act will not be biased by local influence" — hardly the recommendation he would give if a settlement already existed there.

Much changed over the winter of 1897-98. When Captain Ray mushed up the Yukon River from Fort Yukon to Dawson City at the end of February 1898, many disgruntled Americans (unable to find stakeable claims and unhappy with Canadian regulations) were headed back to the U.S.. Ray found miners camped at Mission Creek and Seventymile River (about 10 miles downriver from Mission Creek). Because of the beneficial attributes of the Mission Creek site, he still recommended building a military post there.

In May of that year a group of 28 miners laid out a townsite at Mission Creek, calling their new town Eagle City (because of eagles nesting on the bluffs just to the north). By summer there were about 500 cabins and 1,700 residents.

A sawmill quickly sprang up and three commercial companies built stores: Alaska Commercial, North American Transportation and Trading, and Alaska Exploration Company. The new city soon boasted a hospital, newspaper, several churches and numerous saloons.

Eagle became the first incorporated city in Interior Alaska in January 1901, and residents designated the log cabin pictured in the drawing as City Hall. Located at 1901 Chamberlain Street near St. Paul's Church and the river, it was built with round logs saddle-notched at the corners, and has a corrugated metal roof. A 1986 addition to the rear is also constructed of logs and blends nicely with the older structure. Still used as City Hall, it is typical of many Eagle buildings.

Sources:

- Architectural data form for City of Eagle city hall. Sandra Faulkner. *Historic American Buildings Survey,* National Park Service. 1986
- *Eagle-Fort Egbert, A Remnant of the Past.* no author. U.S. Bureau of Land Management. 1999
- *Fort Egbert and Eagle, a preservation plan.* no author. National Trust for Historic Preservation. 1976
- *Recollections of the Youkon: Memoires from the Years 1868-1885.* F. X. Mercier. Alaska Historical Commission. 1986
- "Relief of the Destitute in the Gold Fields." Captain P. H. Ray. May 5, 1898 report in *Compilation of Narratives of Explorations in Alaska, United States Congress, Senate Committee on Military Affairs.* 1900
- *Yukon, The Last Frontier: A History of the Yukon Basin of Canada and Alaska.* Melody Webb. University of New Mexico Press. 1985

Taylor Highway - Eagle

Eagle NC Co. store in 1999

## Northern Commercial Company helped city of Eagle survive

If you have an eye for detail the front door is a giveaway. Otherwise, glancing at Eagle's old Northern Commercial Company (NC Co.) store, shown in the drawing, you might be deceived into thinking it is a small structure. However, those seemingly four-foot tall windows along the front of the building are actually eight feet tall. Instead of being 12 feet wide, the building it is about 24 feet wide and about 60 feet long, with 10-foot ceilings.

The tall front windows, and transom window over the centrally-placed front door, which allowed as much light as possible inside, are typical of commercial buildings built across the United States in the early 1900s. There are no side windows except at the back of the building since the walls would have been lined with floor-to-ceiling shelves.

The NC Co. (at the turn of the 20th century it was the Alaska Commercial Company) built a store at Eagle in 1898, shortly after the community was established, while the Klondike Gold Rush was in full stride. Although the Dawson City area was a major gold producer, many U.S. miners, disgruntled with Canadian regulations and unable to find claims to stake, had returned to diggings on the U.S. side of the border, establishing numerous mining camps along the Yukon River between Eagle and Circle. Many of these camps had patriotic names such as Nation, Independence, Eagle and Star City.

Eagle became a commercial and government center. A U.S. Army installation (Fort Egbert) was built there, and the town became headquarters for the Third Judicial District. Three major trading companies opened stores: The NC Co., North American Trading Company, and the Alaska Exploration Company.

According to the book, *Flag over the North, the story of the Northern Commercial Company*, the first NC Co. store in Eagle was a large log structure located on B Street, a few hundred yards from the river. Sometime before 1905 the log store was replaced with the current wood-frame building.

When the Third Judicial District moved its headquarters to Fairbanks in 1903 as the Klondike Gold Rush waned, the future of Eagle dimmed considerably. However, mining techniques learned in the Klondike, such as hydraulicking and dredging, opened up new areas in Alaska.

The book, *Yukon, the Last Frontier*, states that by 1916 there were 70 mines in the Circle-Eagle area, and in the 1930s and early 1940s the region supported seven gold dredges. Because of its location and already existing infrastructure, Eagle became a regional support center.

The NC Co. was the major trading company along the lower Yukon River. At its zenith, it owned 22 stores from Eagle near the Canadian border to St. Michael near the mouth of the river on Norton Sound. In addition to its stores, the NC Co. also operated a river navigation company, as did the two other trading companies in Eagle.

Over time, as Klondike mining ebbed, the NC Co. absorbed some competitors and forced others out of business. Eventually it became the sole trading company in Eagle, owning a handful of storefronts and warehouses.

Preservation plans for the Fort Egbert and Eagle Historic District indicate that by 1915 the NC Co. had centralized its store operations to a building it had acquired along the riverfront. Although the company still owned the B Street building, it was used for a time as a restaurant.

The NC Co. closed its Eagle operations in the 1950s and the B Street building sat vacant for years. It was acquired by the city in 1968 and later purchased by Steve Nelson, an Eagle resident. Another Eagle resident, John Borg, told me that Mr. Nelson has stabilized the building by putting in a new concrete foundation. Although it is currently only used for storage, it remains an important part of Eagle's history and a rare example of early Interior Alaska commercial buildings.

Sources:

- Conversation with John Borg, Eagle resident and Historic Eagle tour guide . 2014
- *Flag over the North, the story of the Northern Commercial Company*. L. D. Kitchener. Superior Publishing. 1954
- *Fort Egbert and Eagle, a Preservation Plan*. National Trust for Historic Preservation, for U.S. Bureau of Land Management. 1976
- *Yukon, The Last Frontier: A History of the Yukon Basin of Canada and Alaska*. Melody Webb. University of New Mexico Press. 1985

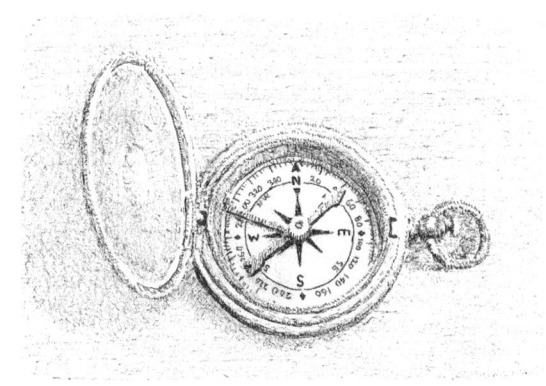

Tagylor Highway - Eagle

Roald Amundsen cabin in 2012

## Roald Amundsen cabin in Eagle - a link with bygone era of Polar exploration

The small frame house shown in the drawing, located in Eagle, Alaska, is where Norwegian explorer Roald Amundsen (1872-1928) spent several months during the winter of 1905-06. He had mushed to Eagle, 400 miles south of the Arctic Ocean where Amundsen's iced-in boat lay anchored, to send a telegram announcing that he and his crew were the first explorers to successfully sail through the Northwest Passage, the fabled ocean route traversing the Canadian Archipelago.

In contrast to earlier unsuccessful expeditions that involved large ships, scores of men, and dependence on tons of supplies carried onboard, Amundsen sailed a small shallow-draft boat with an appropriately small crew, and as much as possible lived off the resources of the area. He and his hand-picked six-man crew set sail on June 16, 1903 from Christiana (Oslo), Norway aboard the 70' sloop Gjoa.

Several months later he sailed into the Canadian Archipelago northwest of Hudson's Bay, searching for a location to set up scientific instruments to study the North Magnetic Pole. Aided by a group of Netsilik Inuit who settled nearby, Amundsen spent two winters at a site he christened Gjoahavn, in a protected harbor on the southeastern coast of King William Island.

During that time his party conducted systematic magnetic and meteorological observations at Gjoahavn, and made forays to map the local area and take observations closer to the magnetic pole. One of the important discoveries from the expedition was that the pole had shifted about 30 miles to the north since first being located in 1831.

After his second winter at Gjoahavn, Amundsen continued his quest to navigate the Northwest Passage. Guided part way by Inuit kayakers, the Gjoa inched through the shallow, island-dotted waters until finally reaching Herschel Island in the eastern Beaufort Sea. Because of the all-too-short navigation season, Amundsen was forced to overwinter there, along with several whaling vessels which had been plying the Arctic Ocean near the Bering Straits.

A wrecked whaling schooner was beached at Point King, near where the Gjoa was anchored. According to the book, "Amundsen, the splendid Norseman," the ship's captain wanted to reach San Francisco to outfit another ship for the next whaling season and contracted with Inuit guides to take him by dog sled as far as Fort Yukon.

Amundsen agreed to accompany them on the trip. Being the good Norwegian he was, Amundsen skied much of the way, helping break trail for the sled dogs. Some accounts stress Amundsen's desire to send word of his success back to Norway, but Elva Scott, in a 1996 Fairbanks Daily News-Miner article, wrote that he was also seeking medical assistance for an ill crew member.

Fort Yukon did not have the telegraph facility that Amundsen had hoped for, so he and the whaling captain decided to push on to Eagle while their Inuit guides waited for Amundsen's return at Fort Yukon.

When Amundsen arrived in Eagle on December 5, 1905 the thermometer read -60 degrees F. Amundsen's first stop was the Northern Commercial Company (NC Co.) store, where he was mistaken for just another bedraggled prospector until asking to send a telegram to Norway. Broke, he had to send the 3,000 word telegram collect.

While waiting for replies to his telegram and for funds to complete his voyage, Amundsen lived in Eagle as guest of the NC Company's store manager, Frank Smith. The small gable-roofed cabin he stayed in, about 15' square with a small shed-roofed rear extension, is located on what is now called Amundsen Street, behind the old NC. Co. store building.

Amundsen finally departed Eagle on February 3, 1906, skiing the 400 miles back to the Gjoa. Later that year he and his crew completed their historic voyage across the Arctic Ocean, arriving at Nome in the Bering Straits on September 1, 1906.

Sources:

- "Amundsen Cabin." Sandra Faulkner. *Historic American Buildings Survey*, National Park Service. 1986
- *Amundsen, the splendid Norseman*. Bellamy Partridge. Frederick A. Stokes Company. 1929
- "Arctic explorer leaves imprint in Eagle." Elva Scott. in *Fairbanks Daily News-Miner*. 10-6-1996
- *The North West Passage; the 'Gjöa' expedition*, 1903-1907. Roald Amundsen. E. Dutton. 1908
- *The Last Viking, the life of Roald Amundsen*. Stephen R. Brown. Da Capo Press. 2012

Old Chicken schoolhouse in 1999

## Tisha's schoolhouse and old town of Chicken, still attract visitors

The first time we visited Chicken in the 1990s there was little you could see from the Taylor highway. Downtown Chicken (adjacent to the highway) had a saloon, cafe and small store. There may have been a gas station—I don't remember.

The highway skirts the south edge of the old townsite, and if you didn't know old town was there, you might drive by and not notice. However, we had read Anne Purdy's book, *Tisha*, about her first year as a teacher in Chicken, had even gone to college with one of Anne's daughters, and knew of old Chicken. One of our goals was to find the old schoolhouse, shown in the drawing.

Chicken is in the heart of a mountainous, isolated region through which the Fortymile River tumbles from its headwaters in Alaska to its confluence with the Yukon River in Canada, forty miles downriver from Fort Reliance, near

Dawson City. A combination of rough trail and wagon road from Eagle to the north (only 55 miles by air, but 90 miles by pack train) was the community's primary surface link for almost 50 years.

The region, home to Han Kutchin Athabascans for thousands of years, began to attract prospectors in the late 1800s. Gold was discovered along the Fortymile River in 1886 and the town of Fortymile sprang up at the river's mouth (which miners thought was in the U.S.).

Pierre Berton, in his book *Klondike, the Last Great Gold Rush,* said the men attracted to the region appeared to be chasing their fortune, but "…seemed more like men pursued than men pursuing, and if they sought anything, it was the right to be left alone." Berton goes on to describe Fortymile as "…a community of hermits whose one common bond was their mutual isolation."

Prospectors found gold along Chicken Creek (on the U.S. side of the border) in 1891 and a town formed around the claims. In her book, Anne relates two possibilities for how Chicken got its name. The first is that miners wanted to name the community after the abundant Ptarmigan in the area, but no one was sure of the spelling so they settled on calling the town Chicken. The other possibility is that gold found in the area was commonly about the size of kernels of corn—i.e. chicken feed.

A post office was established in 1903 and three years later the two-story Chicken Creek Hotel was constructed. The town's heyday was between 1910 and the mid 1920s, when, according to census data, about 100 people lived in the immediate area. During this period Chicken served as a supply center for surrounding creeks.

Alaska's territorial government took over the Chicken Creek Hotel building in 1924. It tore the second story down and converted the building into a schoolhouse.

The re-purposed building had two rooms in the front of the 25' x 32' squared-log structure. One of the front doors led to the teacher's quarters, and the other opened into the classroom. Storage rooms were located in the back.

Chicken's population had started to decline by 1927 when Anne (called Tisha by a young Native student who couldn't pronounce teacher) arrived to teach school, and shrinking enrollment forced the school to close the next year.

After the school closed it became a roadhouse for a number of years. The Fairbanks Exploration Company bought up the land and buildings in and around the community in the 1940s, and in 1959 it moved a dredge to the area. The dredge operated until 1967, using the old town as a support camp.

When the F.E. Company stopped mining, it sold the camp and dredge, which are now tourist attractions. A handful of people still live in Chicken year-round, and the area's population swells during summer when miners come to work their claims, and tourists (bound for Eagle, Dawson City, and Tok) drive through. And there are still more than a few who come specifically to see the old town and Tisha's schoolhouse.

The old townsite, which is private property, was declared a Historic District in 2001. Tours are conducted in the summer.

Sources:

- "Chicken Historic District, National Register of Historic Places Registration Form." Rogan Faith. National Park Service. 2001
- *Cultural Resource Survey of the Taylor Highway.* Rolfe Buzzell. Alaska Department of Natural Resources. 2003
- *Klondike, the Last Great Gold Rush*. Pierre Berton. McLelland and Stewart. 1958
- *They didn't come in Four-Wheel Drives, An Introduction to Fortymile History*. Terry Haynes. U.S. Bureau of Land Management. 1976
- *Tisha*. Anne Hobbs Purdy. St. Martins Press. 1976
- *Yukon, the Last Frontier*. Melody Webb. University of Nebraska Press. 1985

Chicken dredge in 1999

# From Fairbanks to Chicken, a long road for FE Company's Dredge No. 4

The Fairbanks Exploration Company's (FE Co.) Dredge No. 4 (also called the Pedro dredge) in Chicken originally operated along Pedro Creek just north of Fairbanks.

Built by the Yuba Manufacturing Company in California for the FE Co., it was shipped to Fairbanks from Oakland in the spring of 1938. Assembled at Pedro Creek, it began churning the creek's gravels on July 11, 1938. The dredge was specifically designed to extract gold from the shallow gravels along Pedro Creek and was the company's smallest dredge, utilizing 3-cubic-foot buckets. (Most of the FE Company's dredges had 6- or 10-cubic-foot buckets.)

By the 1950s the FE Co. realized Dredge No. 4 would soon exhaust Pedro Creek's gravel and made plans to move the dredge to new ground. Back in 1939-40, the company had acquired claims about 200 miles to the east, along Mosquito Fork and Chicken Creek (tributaries of the South Fork of the Fortymile River), as well as a small steam-powered dredge on Mosquito Fork that had been operated by the Alaska Gold Dredging Company.

According to the 1996 U.S. Geological Survey publication, *Gold Placers of the Historical Fortymile River Region*, the Mosquito Fork dredge had been shipped in pieces from Skagway to Whitehorse on the White Pass and Yukon Railroad, and then transported by riverboat down the Yukon to the mouth of the Fortymile River. From there it was skidded during winter behind caterpillar tractors up the Fortymile to Mosquito Fork. And after all that effort it only operated about a year and a half.

The FE Co. contemplated renovating the Mosquito Fork Dredge for use on Chicken Creek, but with the opening of the Taylor Highway in 1953, decided instead to move its No. 4 dredge from Fairbanks to Chicken. No. 4's hull design of welded steel pontoons allowed it to be transported in sections, and coupled with the dredge's compact design, it was less costly to disassemble and truck it from Fairbanks to Chicken than to renovate the Mosquito Fork dredge.

No. 4 was disassembled and trucked to Chicken in 1958, re-assembled, and put into operation in 1959. The dredge had originally been supplied with electrical power from the FE Co.'s Fairbanks power plant. At its new remote location two diesel engines were installed onboard to provide electricity.

The dredge operated until 1967, when diminishing gold recovery and operational problems forced the company to permanently shut down operations. The dredge was "parked" on a ledge of bedrock, its buckets removed, and its doors and windows shuttered. The book, *The Northern Gold Fleet: Twentieth-century Gold Dredging in Alaska*, relates that No. 4 recovered more than $2 million in gold and silver during its nine years at Chicken.

The dredge sat on the tailings along Chicken Creek until 1998, when Alaska Gold Company (the successor to the FE Co.) sold the dredge to private investors. No. 4 had been sitting north of the Taylor Highway, and its new owners owned property south of the highway, so (in a not-so-simple operation) they jacked up the dredge, put huge trailers under it, and inched it a mile south across the highway. The drawing shows the dredge a year after the move (notice the still-shuttered windows).

After being moved, the dredge's principal owner, Mike Busby, fixed up No. 4 and opened it to the public. The dredge was relocated again in 2009, but this time movers constructed and filled a pond around the dredge, floating it to its new home.

Busby and his partners also acquired all the equipment and parts associated with the dredge's operation, including the dredge's buckets. Because of this, and the fact that its remote location discouraged souvenir hunters, it is one of the most complete dredges in Alaska. Busby told me that it would actually take very little to make the dredge operational. Dredge No. 4 is open to the public every summer.

Sources:

- Correspondence with Mike Busby, owner of Dredge No. 4. 2014
- "F.E. Company Dredge No. 4 National Register of Historic Places Nomination Form." Michael Busby. National Park Service. 2006
- *Gold Placers of the Historical Fortymile River Region*, U.S.G.S. Survey Bulletin 2125. Warren Yeend. U.S. Geological Survey. 1996
- *History of Alaska Operations of Unites States Smelting, Refining and Mining Company*. John Boswell. Mineral Industries Research Laboratory, University of Alaska, Fairbanks. 1979
- *The Northern Gold Fleet: Twentieth-Century Gold Dredging in Alaska*. Clark C. Spence. University of Illinois Press. 1996

Fortymile Roadhouse in 1998

# The Fortymile Roadhouse – gateway to the historic Fortymile country

The 160-mile long Taylor Highway was constructed between 1947 and 1951 to connect the Alaska Highway with the Fortymile River region (often referred to as "Fortymile country") and the city of Eagle on the Yukon River.

When the road was proposed and during construction, it was referred to as simply the "Fortymile Road." It was later named the Taylor Highway in honor of Ike Taylor, Alaska Road Commission (ARC) president from 1932-1948.

During the early 1900s, the ARC constructed a road from Eagle as far south as Wade Creek, a distance of about 60 miles. At the same time, the government of Canada's Yukon Territory extended its road system westward from Dawson to serve miners in the Sixty Mile River area. In the 1930s the ARC and Yukon Territory linked their two roads, and the Top of the World Highway (Yukon Highway 9) was born.

According to articles appearing in the *Fairbanks Daily News-Miner* in November and December of 1938, the Fairbanks Chamber of Commerce began pushing for a road from Fairbanks to Fortymile country soon after completion of the Top of the World Highway. Chamber members believed that such a road would relieve the "shut-in" atmosphere of the Fortymile area and open up opportunities just as the Steese and Elliott highways had done.

Although the ARC was in favor of the road, budget constraints kept the road on the drawing board until World War II intervened and construction efforts were diverted to the Alcan Highway. However, construction of the Alcan accomplished part of what the ARC wanted to do anyway; build over 100 miles of road to the edge of Fortymile country.

The gateway to Fortymile country turned out to be just a few miles east of the new community of Tok. When the Alcan was built, land ownership was not a prime consideration, and the section of highway just east of Tok ended up passing through the northern edge of the Tetlin Native Reserve, one of the few reservations ever established in Alaska. The new junction of the Alcan Highway and the Fortymile Road was about 13 miles north of the Athabascan village of Tetlin, so it was naturally called Tetlin Junction.

Seizing the opportunity to be the first business serving the new road, Ray and Mable Scoby, along with their partner, Clarence "Red" Post, decided to build the Fortymile Roadhouse at the junction. According to a Bureau of Land Management report, "Indians, Traders and Bureaucrats in the Upper Tanana District; a History of the Tetlin Reserve," they leased land from the Bureau of Indian Affairs and began building in 1948, before the road was completed.

Roy David Sr., an Athabascan who grew up in Tetlin, said in a 2013 interview that when he went to work for the Scobys in 1952, only the café was open. Over time the Scobys added a bathhouse, numerous tiny rental cabins located in front of the bathhouse, and a service station with garage to repair vehicles. The drawing shows the café and bathhouse. Ray Scoby also operated a small sawmill processing timber he harvested under permit from the Tetlin reserve. After thirty years of operation, the Scoby's sold the roadhouse in 1978.

Tok is only about 12 miles away, and as highway conditions improved and new visitor facilities were built in Tok, there was less need for the roadhouse at Tetlin Junction. The roadhouse finally closed in about 1985 but opened again briefly in 1992 for the 50th anniversary of the Alaska Highway.

The drawing shows the roadhouse in 1998 when the buildings were still in decent shape. Now, the rental units have disappeared and everything else is boarded up, weathering away amid obscuring trees.

Sources:

- "Chamber of Commerce endorses Fortymile Road." in *Fairbanks Daily News-Miner*. 11-15-38
- "Driving along Alaska highways." in *Fairbanks Daily News-Miner*. 5-25-73
- "Indians, Traders and Bureaucrats in the Upper Tanana District: A History of the Tetlin Reserve." C. Michael Brown. U.S. Bureau of Land Management. 1984
- "Lack of Fortymile Road gives rich district dim, shut-in atmosphere." in *Fairbanks Daily News-Miner*. 12-7-1938
- "Roy David Sr. Oral History." interview by Barbara Cellarius and Leslie McCartney. Oral History Collection, University of Alaska Fairbanks Archives. 2013
- "Tok-to-Border folks feel like second-class citizens." in *Fairbanks Daily News Miner*. 4-11-1963

Alaska Highway - Northway Junction

Old Civil Aeronautics Administration truck near Northway in 2011

# 1942 CAA truck and Northway Airfield - parts of Alaska's aviation history

The vehicle in the drawing is a 1942 GMC dump truck sitting on a hillside at about 1620 Mile of the Alaska Highway. Stenciled on the door is "Department of Commerce, Civil Aeronautics Administration." The CAA was the precursor to the Federal Aviation Administration, and this truck (probably surplus Alaska Highway construction equipment) was undoubtedly used at the Northway airfield just a few miles away.

Northway's airfield was one of the links in the "Northwest Staging Route," through which thousands of aircraft were ferried from the U.S. to the Soviet Union during World War II. Although it was used during the war's lend-lease program, the airfield was actually built a year before the aircraft ferrying operation came into being.

Canada entered World War II in September 1939. The Canadian government was primarily concerned with the war in Europe and the Atlantic, but it did begin planning for a series of airfields stretching from northern Alberta to Whitehorse in the Yukon Territory.

According to Stan Cohen's book, *The Forgotten War, a Pictorial History of World War II in Alaska and Northwestern Canada,* after the Canadian-American Permanent Joint Board on Defense was created in August 1940, Canada authorized construction of airfields at Grande Prairie, Alberta; Fort St. John and Fort Nelson, British Columbia; and Watson Lake and Whitehorse, Yukon Territory.

These airfields were to "provide protection, permit aircraft to be deployed rapidly…in times of emergency, and allow men and supplies to be moved into the region by air." Canada constructed the airfields during 1941, the same year the Northway airfield was built.

The United States began beefing up its northern defenses in 1940. As part of this buildup, the CAA upgraded facilities at numerous airports and constructed additional airfields across the territory.

In Eastern Interior Alaska it built new airfields at Big Delta, Tanacross, and Northway.(The hanger built at the Tanacross airfield is now the Big Dipper ice arena in Fairbanks, and the airfield near Big Delta is now Fort Greely.)

Work on the Northway airfield started before construction of the Alaska Highway, so the site of the proposed airfield was as isolated as the nearby Athabascan village of Northway, after which the airfield was named.

The nearest road and airstrip were about 60 miles to the south near the headwaters of the Nabesna River, at the Nabesna Gold Mine. The Nabesna landing strip became the staging site for shipping supplies to the new airfield.

Supplies were trucked approximately 225 miles from Valdez to the mine. The route followed the Richardson Highway north as far as Gulkana Junction, then northeast to Slana along a road that followed a section of the old Valdez-Eagle Trail, and then southeast along the mine road. From the mine everything was hauled by tractor to the landing strip.

Morrison Knutson Company (MK) was the primary contractor, and it sub-contacted with pioneer Alaska aviator Bob Reeve and others to airlift supplies. Beth Romulo describes the operation in her book, *Glacier Pilot*.

The first task MK faced was blazing a rough airstrip at the proposed airfield. Reeve flew two engineers into the Native village of Tetlin on Tetlin Lake (southeast of present-day Tok) then chartered a motorboat down the Tetlin River and up the Tanana and Nabesna Rivers to the construction site. They hired 20 Athabascan laborers who hacked an 800-foot airstrip out of the wilderness.

With the airstrip in place, Reeve and other pilots began an almost non-stop airlift of supplies. Between June and October of 1941 they flew about 1,000 tons of supplies and 300 workmen to the new airfield. In addition, MK ran a cat-train along the Nabesna River to haul in scrapers and other heavy equipment. By the end of 1941 the airfield was operational.

It is still used today. U.S. Customs has an office at the airport, and small private airplanes entering Alaska from the Whitehorse area in Canada must land there.

Sources:

- *The Forgotten War, a Pictorial History of World War II in Alaska and Northwestern Canada, Volumes One and Two*. Stan Cohen. Pictorial Histories Publishing Company. 1981, 1988
- *Nabesna Gold and the Making of the Historic Nabesna Gold Mine and Town*. Kirk Stanley. Todd Communications. 2005
- *Glacier Pilot; the story of Bob Reeve and the flyers who pushed back Alaska's air frontiers*. Beth Day Romulo. Henry Holt. 1957

Richardson Highway - Delta Junction

Sullivan Roadhouse in 2000

## Sullivan Roadhouse finds rebuilt life in Delta Junction

John and Florence Sullivan (veterans of the Klondike, Nome and Fairbanks gold rushes) built a sod-roofed log roadhouse during the winter of 1905-06 midway along the Donnelly-Washburn Cut-off. It was a Valdez-Fairbanks Trail winter shortcut that crossed the Tanana River near Birch Lake and ran southeast to the Delta River, bypassing Big Delta and slicing 35 miles off the regular trail.

The Sullivan Roadhouse began as a 20-foot by 60-foot "dogtrot" cabin. Common in the southern United States, dogtrot cabins consisted of two separate structures with a breezeway or "dogtrot" between them — all sheltered beneath a common roof.

According to Delta Junction resident Jeff Durham, Alaska's version of the dogtrot allowed mushers to pull into the sheltered breezeway, unhook their dogs and leave the sled.

After one winter of use, the Alaska Road commission (ARC) realigned the winter cut-off to avoid several steep grades, stranding the Sullivan Roadhouse four miles off the trail. Undeterred, the Sullivans disassembled the roadhouse, hauled the logs to the new trail location and rebuilt the structure. This time they added a metal roof, uncommon in early roadhouses.

After the move, the dogtrot was enclosed and became the roadhouse's front room. Later a 13-foot kitchen addition (in the drawing foreground) was tacked on to the end of the building. The roadhouse as pictured in photographs taken around 1910 is similar to what it looks like today. A cabin directly behind and perpendicular to the roadhouse (used as guest quarters), barn, blacksmith shop, cold storage cellar and outhouse completed the roadhouse complex.

The Sullivan Roadhouse was one of the most popular along the Valdez-Fairbanks Trail. Margaret Murie, in her book, *Two in the Far North*, described a 1918 stop at the roadhouse thusly, "The house was low and sprawling, so comfortable looking, larger than the others so far, with a wing extending out at the back. Pa Sullivan himself and a barnman came out to greet us looking well-fed, rosy of face, both in shirtsleeves ... Ma was at the door, neat, roly-poly, pretty in a gingham dress." (Evidently everyone called the Sullivans Ma and Pa.) Margaret goes on to describe the roadhouse as so comfortable and fancy, "that a man of the Trail would be afraid to sit down and relax, but cozy, a home."

With steady improvements to the main trail the winter cut-off received less and less traffic, and after the Alaska Railroad was completed, winter traffic disappeared completely. Ma and Pa Sullivan abandoned the roadhouse in 1922.

The roadhouse lay vacant for much of the next 70 years. All the outbuildings moldered away after their sod roofs rotted and collapsed, exposing their interiors to the elements. The roadhouse building survived though, primarily because of its metal roofing.

The land around the roadhouse was eventually annexed into Fort Greely, and the Army made some repairs to the building, using it during maneuvers. However, the building was adjacent to the Army's Oklahoma Bombing Range, and in the 1990s local historians, the Bureau of Land Management and the Army decided to relocate the roadhouse.

In 1997 the building was disassembled, the pieces lifted by helicopter to Delta Junction, and then reassembled, this time on a new concrete foundation. The bottom three courses of logs were replaced, reproduction doors manufactured, windows re-glazed, new metal roofing installed, and the entire structure refurbished.

The building, now the Sullivan Roadhouse Historical Museum, sits next to the Delta Junction Visitor Center. Dedicated to telling the story of the Valdez-Fairbanks Trail and its roadhouses, the museum is owned and operated by the Delta Junction Chamber of Commerce, which has worked diligently to make the museum a first-class visitor attraction.

Sources:

- Conversation with Jeff Durham, volunteer at Sullivan Roadhouse Museum. 2013
- "National Register of Historic Places Inventory,. Erica Kracker & Edward Kiker. National Park Service. 1978
- "Sullivan Roadhouse." *Historic American Building Survey,* National Park Service. No date (c 1985)
- "Sullivan's Roadhouse Restoration Completed." No author. In *Association for Historic Preservation Newsletter*. Sept. 1996
- *The Trail, the Story of the Historic Valdez-Fairbanks Trail*. Kenneth Marsh. Trapper Creek Museum. 2008
- *Two in the Far North*. Margaret Murie. Alfred A. Knopf. 1962

Rika's Roadhouse in early winter 2011

## Rika's Roadhouse still important fixture along Richardson Highway

Big Delta—so named because of its location at the confluence of the Delta and Tanana Rivers, and to differentiate it from Delta Telegraph Station on the nearby Little Delta River, became one of the most important communities along the Valdez-Fairbanks Trail during the first half of the 20th century. At the height of its importance, it boasted a roadhouse, ferry crossing, telegraph station and steamboat landing, and it sat at the juncture of two trails: the main Valdez Fairbanks Trail, and the Grundler-Tanacross Trail that headed towards the headwaters of the Tanana River.

Ben Bennett built a log trading post near the Valdez-Fairbanks Trail in 1904 on the south bank of the Tanana River, to the east of where Rika's Roadhouse is know. Dan McCarty bought the operation from Bennett the next year, and even though McCarty left in 1906, the site was called McCarty's (or McCarthy's) for almost 30 years.

The Washington-Alaska Military Cable and Telegraph System (WAMCATS) built a telegraph station there in 1907, and since small steamboats could navigate up the Tanana River that far, the station became a transshipment point for supplies headed to telegraph stations further east. Riverboats could also provision McCarty's trading post.

John Hajdukovich, a Serbian immigrant who had moved from Fairbanks to Big Delta in 1906, bought McCarty's trading post in 1909. This was about the same time that the Alaska Road Commission (ARC) upgraded the Valdez-Fairbanks trail to a wagon road.

That same year Hajdukovich built the first section of a roadhouse—a substantial 2 ½-story log structure. That original section, still the main part of Rika's Roadhouse, is 31'9" wide by 43'2" long and is built of round spruce logs.

According to Bureau of Land Management reports, Hajdukovich became one of the dominant freighters and trading post operators in Eastern Interior Alaska. He had trading posts at Healy Lake, Tanacross, Tetlin and Northway; and operated a small fleet of gasoline-powered freight boats. However, because of all his other activities it appears he was an indifferent roadhouse operator and offered minimal services at his Big Delta establishment. The National Register of Historic Places registration form for the Big Delta Historic District states that travelers even had to cook their own meals.

In about 1919 he hired Rika Wallen (born Erika Yakobsen in Wallen, Sweden) to help at the roadhouse. In 1923 he sold the Roadhouse to her and it was rechristened Rika's Roadhouse. She added a 2 ½-story wing to the roadhouse in 1926. The 20' x 40' addition was built by Louis Grimsmore using squared spruce logs.

Rika also built a barn, springhouse, windmill, and several outbuildings. She cultivated an extensive garden; raised sheep, goats and chickens; and grew grain to feed her animals. Her roadhouse quickly developed into an informal headquarters for area trappers, prospectors and hunters, and also served travelers along the trail.

The Valdez-Fairbanks Trail eventually became the Richardson highway, and a 1928 brochure promoting the Richardson described Rika's as "one of the most important centers of trade along the road, being the supply point for the inhabitants of the entire region of the headwaters of the Tanana River….Here also is located a commodious roadhouse boasting of such luxuries as fresh milk and domestic fowls…as well as all kinds of wild meats, berries, fish, etc."

As with a few other roadhouses along the Valdez-Fairbanks Trail, a realignment of the road forced Rika's out of business. The Army built a temporary bridge across the Tanana River in 1942, which was replaced in 1943 by a steel bridge built by the Alaska Road Commission. Now bypassed by the highway, Rika closed the roadhouse in 1947 but continued to live in the area until her death in 1969.

The roadhouse lay empty and decaying for years, until the State of Alaska acquired the property and buildings in 1976 and developed the site into Big Delta State Historical Park. During the 1980s, the roadhouse and several other buildings at the site were restored.

The buildings are closed during the winter, but visitors can explore the park year-round.

Sources:

- "Big Delta Historic District, National Register of Historic Places Registration Form." Judith Bittner. National Park Service. 1991
- "Rika's Landing Roadhouse, National Register of Historic Places Inventory-Nomination Form." Alfred Mongin, National Park Service. 1976
- *Roadhouses of the Richardson Highway.* Walter Phillips. Alaska Historical Commission. 1984
- *The Trail, the Story of the Historic Valdez-Fairbanks Trail.* Kenneth Marsh. Trapper Creek Museum. 2008
- "Tanana River Navigability Report." Ralph Basner. U.S. Bureau of Land Management. 2002

Ferryman's cabin at Big Delta in 2012

## Alaska Road Commission's Big Delta ferry – of roads, truckers and tolls

When the Alaska Road Commission (ARC) was created in 1905, it undertook the herculean task of building roads and trails throughout the Territory.

One of its first projects was upgrading the winter-only Valdez-Fairbanks Trail to a year-round wagon road. With limited funds and manpower the ARC avoided building bridges along the trail if at all possible. Small streams were simply forded and larger ones crossed with wooden culverts constructed on site.

The preferred alternative for crossing large rivers during the ARC's early years was by ferry. Ken Marsh's book, *The Trail, the story of the historic Valdez-Fairbanks Trail*, lists four ferry-crossings along the route: over Chena Slough; and across the Salcha, Tanana, and Tazlina Rivers.

A cable-ferry across the Tanana River was installed at Big Delta in 1909. No motor was needed for the ferry since its hull design and steering allowed the river current to propel the craft.

Over the next few years road improvements allowed motor vehicles to begin replacing horse-drawn wagons. A 1915 report records that the ferry could accommodate two Model T Fords, or a single four-horse wagon.

The ferryman's cabin at Big Delta (shown in the drawing) was constructed in 1929 by Louis Grimsmore. (He also constructed the 1926 addition to Rika's Roadhouse.) The cabin is made of peeled logs, and is 14' 9" wide by 18' long, with 6-foot eaves extending over the door. A 1930s photo in the UAF Archives shows the cabin much as it appears today, except with a sod roof.

Bridges gradually replaced ferries along the route, but the Tanana River ferry still operated up through the 1930s. This meant that Big Delta was a chokepoint along the trail, a situation the ARC took advantage of starting in 1935 when the federal government sought to collect tolls from road users. This was partly to equalize costs between motor freight carriers and the government-owned Alaska Railroad so the highway wouldn't divert traffic from the railroad.

The ARC set up vehicle scales at Big Delta and began charging truckers 2.5 cents per mile per ton to cross the river. Truckers vehemently opposed the toll. Some sporadically blocked the ferry approach, others temporarily commandeered the facility. They eventually set up a competing ferry, flying the skull and crossbones as they crossed the river. In response the ARC set up a toll gate at the Shaw Creek bridge, but truckers tore it down.

Several truckers were arrested and a few even prosecuted, but no Fairbanks jury would convict them. Claus-M. Naske wrote in his book, *Alaska Road Commission Historical Narration*, that (regarding the trial of truckers for commandeering the ferry) "most Fairbanksans considered taking the ferry as a protest against the toll as a type of 'Boston Tea Party patriotism.'"

World War II brought an end to the escalating dilemma by filling Alaska Railroad cars with freight and personnel headed for war-time construction projects. Goods moving along the Richardson Highway no longer mattered and tolls were quickly eliminated.

The war brought other changes along the Richardson as well. The newly constructed Alaska Highway connected with the Richardson a few miles from Big Delta.

Wanting unimpeded access to the military facilities in Fairbanks, the Army eliminated the Tanana River ferry by building a temporary wooden bridge across the river in 1942. Spring break-up in 1943 destroyed the bridge, but the ARC constructed a steel-truss bridge across the river the same year and realigned the highway, bypassing both the ferry and Rika's Roadhouse.

After the State of Alaska acquired the ferry location in 1976 as part of the Big Delta State Historical Park project, it renovated the scales and ferryman's cabin. The cabin's foundation, floor, and the first three courses of logs were replaced. Its sod roof (by then covered with metal roofing) was removed and new roof decking and rolled-roofing installed. The cabin now serves as a reminder of the ARC's early and occasionally contentious history.

Sources:

- *Alaska Road Commission Historical Narrative – Final Report*. Claus-M. Naske. State of Alaska. 1983
- "Big Delta Historic District, National Register of Historic Places Registration Form." Judith Bittner. National Park Service. 1991
- *Paving Alaska's trails, the work of the Alaska Road Commission*. Claus-M. Naske. University Press of America. 1986
- T*he Trail, the Story of the Historic Valdez-Fairbanks Trail*. Kenneth Marsh. Trapper Creek Museum. 2008
- Woodrow Johansen Papers. University of Alaska Fairbanks Archives

Richardson Highway - Harding Lake

Bingle Camp lodge in 2001

## Bingle Memorial Camp namesake was indefatigable worker

Bingle Memorial Camp is set on a picturesque 66-acre heavily-wooded parcel along the south shore of Harding Lake, about 47 miles southeast of Fairbanks. It exists in large part because of the vision of Bert Bingle, a Presbyterian minister who spent most of his career building churches and church camps throughout Alaska, and traveling thousands of miles to reach his parishioners. Bert was indefatigable, and my wife, who knew the Bingle family, says the only time he slowed down was to get other people to speed up.

Bert and his wife, Mable, came to Alaska in 1928 to serve the residents of Cordova, on the south side of Prince William Sound. Cordova, a small fishing town, was also the terminus of the Copper River and Northwestern Railroad that brought copper to tidewater from the Kennicott copper mine 200 miles inland at McCarthy. In addition to holding services in Cordova, Bert road the train north once a month to conduct services for the miners. (a foretaste of Bert's later railroad ministry).

In 1935, when the Matanuska Colony (a New Deal resettlement project) was established, the Bingles transferred to Palmer and were there to greet the first settlers. Bert did his best to help the colonists feel less isolated and far from home, setting up a short-wave radio for visitors to listen to, and publishing Palmer's first newspaper of sorts—mimeographed sheets printed in the Bingles' cramped tent.

By 1941 the Bingles were on the move again, this time to a railroad and highway ministry along the Alaska Railroad and the Richardson, Glenn and Steese Highways. Based out of their home in College, Bert rode the rails to hold services at Nenana, Healy, McKinley National Park (now Denali National Park and Preserve), and Curry. Referring to his railroad ministry, he liked to tell people that his church was the longest in the world, "225 miles long and six feet wide." He also drove to Ester and Chatanika for services, and several points along the Richardson and Glenn Highways.

When World War II broke out Bert began acting as an unofficial chaplain for personnel located at the Big Delta Army Airfield (now Fort Greely). As construction began on the Alaska Highway, Bert also volunteered to serve the construction camps between Big Delta in Alaska, and Whitehorse in the Yukon Territory.

It was probably on one of Bert's innumerable trips along the Richardson highway that he began toying with the idea of establishing a youth camp at Harding Lake. He had already helped build a youth camp at Kings Lake in the Matanuska Valley, as well as six churches scattered across South Central and Interior Alaska. Building was in his blood.

Bingle Memorial Camp is located about seven miles off the Richardson Highway, almost directly across the lake from the Harding Lake State Recreation Area. When the Presbyterian Church (with Bert in the lead) established the camp in 1953, there wasn't even road access. Bert was instrumental in getting a road punched out to the camp, and for many years that was as far as the road went.

During the 1950s and 60s many of the camp's building were constructed, including the main lodge and residential cabins. One of my wife's older brothers helped build some of the cabins during one summer.

All of these older buildings are of log construction. The camp still maintains its rustic charm, and most of the buildings, including all of the residential cabins and the camp chapel, are unplumbed and heated by wood stoves. The only exceptions are the main lodge (where the kitchen and dining hall are), a modern (fully plumbed) retreat center, and a modern (also fully plumbed) showerhouse.

Several hundred feet above Harding Lake, the lodge has a commanding view. It's a wonderful place to watch the world go by. I have spent many pleasant days there. One year in late Fall I was the only person in camp, chopping wood for an upcoming event. Long vees of sandhill cranes, brilliantly lit by the afternoon sun, flew overhead while down on the lake a raucous gathering of about 100 swans waited for their departure time.

Bingle Memorial Camp is owned by the Presbyterian Church USA, and managed by an inter-denominational board of directors. When camp is not being held, the facilities are available for rent.

Sources:

- *Alaskan Missions, My 28 years in the Yukon Presbytery*. Rev. Bert Bingle. College, Alaska. no date
- "Chaplains have been serving Alaska service members for years." Chaplain (Lt. Col.) Ted McGovern. Joint Base Elmendorf-Richardson website. 2012
- *Footprints, Sketches of 100 Yukon Presbyterians*. no author. Presbytery of the Yukon. 1998
- Conversation with Claude Klaver, retired Presbyterian minister and long-time associate of Bingle Camp. 2013
- Conversation with Betsy Bonnell, retired Bureau of Land Management realty specialist and family friend of the Bingles. 2013

Denali Highway - Maclaren River

Whitey's cabin in 2004

## Denali Highway history and Whitey's cabin at Maclaren River

When the Denali Highway opened in 1957 it was more than just a 135-mile scenic byway between Paxson and Cantwell. It was the only road connecting Mt. McKinley National Park (now Denali National Park and Preserve) to the rest of the territory. Before the highway opened, the primary means to reach the park was the Alaska Railroad

Many Alaskans began pushing for road access to the park in the 1930s. Officials from the Territory and the National Park Service saw the road's potential to boost tourism. Some, like park superintendent Frank Been, also welcomed an alternative to the Alaska Railroad's high fares and hotel rates. (The railroad managed the park hotel then.)

Little was accomplished before the end of World War II. However, the war did bring extension of the Glenn Highway from Southcentral Alaska to the Richardson Highway, and construction of the Alaska Highway, both important to positioning the park as a destination for vacationers.

Efforts to build the Denali road intensified as the war ended. In 1945 the Alaska Road Commission recommended construction of a "Paxson-McKinley Park Road" and started surveying for the project in 1947.

The surveyed route followed parts of existing trails. There were already trails to the mining district at Valdez Creek (just upriver from the Susitna River bridge). Surveyors followed the Paxson-Valdez Creek Trail as far as the Maclaren River Valley in the east, and traced the Cantwell-Valdez Creek Trail as far as Brushkana Creek in the west.

Early 1950 saw road crews breaking ground, working towards each other from Cantwell and Paxson. That fall, construction also began on a road from Cantwell to McKinley Park Station.

By 1952 the 29-mile segment from Cantwell into the park was completed. The same year the Paxson-McKinley Park Road was officially named the Denali Highway.

Construction continued slowly on the rest of the highway. The book, *Crown Jewel of the North: An Administrative History of Denali National Park and Preserve,* relates that work in an area west of the Susitna River was particularly troublesome because of an "obstinate hill that held out for three years despite…continual thawing and scraping… At one time, the mud was so bad that six of the crew's 18 large D-8 'cats' were put out of commission, buried above their tracks."

By 1956 remaining efforts centered on bridge construction and completing the 37 ½-mile segment between the Susitna and Maclaren Rivers. In early August of 1957 the road's two ends were finally connected, and the Denali Highway officially opened on August 5th. However, the first private vehicle to drive the length of the Denali Highway reportedly snuck through on August 2nd.

As hoped, opening the Denali Highway sparked increased tourism. Establishments such as Maclaren River Lodge (42 miles from Paxson) and Gracious House (53 miles from Cantwell) popped up along the remote road to serve travelers.

Built around 1957, Whitey Mathison's cabin (shown in the drawing) was one of the first structures erected at Maclaren River Lodge. Located across the parking lot from the current lodge, it was the cook shack during construction.

The Maclaren River is above timberline, and according to musher John Schandelmeier (who used to live nearby) logs for the lodge were trucked from Delta Junction. Since building logs were at a premium, the 12' x 24' cook's cabin was built with varied materials, lending it an eclectic appearance.

Whitey was the owner of the lodge and lived in the cabin until his death in 1973. Supposedly, the cabin and lodge are haunted by two women rarely seen but sometimes heard talking to each other.

The cabin deteriorated considerably over the years, and in 2009, the current lodge owners, Alan and Susie Echols, rebuilt it. They raised the structure, replaced many of the rotting logs, installed a new roof, and remodeled its interior. Hopefully, Whitey's cabin will continue to provide shelter for visitors at Maclaren River for many years to come.

Sources:

- *An Historical Resource Study of the Valdez Creek Mining District, Alaska*. Peter F. Dessauer & David W. Harvey. U. S. Bureau of Land Management. 1977
- Correspondence with Susie Echols, co-owner of Maclaren River Lodge. 2014
- Correspondence with John Schandelmeier, former resident of Maclaren River area. 2014
- *Crown Jewel of the North: An Administrative History of Denali National Park and Preserve, Volume 1*. Frank Norris. National Park Service. 2006

Denali Highway - Brushkana Creek

Brushkana Creek ARC cabin in 2013

# Brushkana Creek cabin a remnant of Denali transportation history

The Alaska Road Commission (ARC) cabin on Brushkana Creek (shown in drawing) is one of the few remnants of the Cantwell-Valdez Creek Trail.

Bruskana is a clearwater stream that cascades northward out of the Talkeetna Mountains, crossing the Denali Highway and eventually joining the Nenana River. It is a popular recreation destination. Grayling are plentiful, and the creek is floatable from the Bureau of Land Management Brushkana Creek Campground located at the Denali Highway crossing.

During the early 1900s the area was only accessible on foot or horseback. The Alaska Range between Cantwell and the Susitna River was little explored by Westerners, although it had been occupied by Ahtna Athabascans for generations.

A 1903 gold discovery at Valdez Creek near the Susitna River's headwaters (about 55 miles east of Cantwell) caused a minor stampede, but the first trails to the gold regions were from the east, taking off from the Valdez-Fairbanks Trail.

With the completion of the Alaska Railroad as far as Cantwell in 1919, the distance for freighting supplies to Valdez Creek shrank dramatically — 55 miles instead of the 250 miles from Valdez, or 200 miles from the Copper River and Northwestern Railroad at Chitina.

Freighting naturally shifted to the shorter western route. BLM documents state that the Alaska Railroad quickly blazed a year-round trail (pack-horse trains in summer, horse and dog-drawn sleds in winter) to the mines. It ran east from Cantwell along the Nenana River and Brushkana Creek until climbing out of the Nenana River drainage onto the Susitna River flats and then crossing the Susitna to Valdez Creek. In the summer, freight had to be ferried across the river.

The trip from Cantwell to Valdez Creek took three days, and the ARC, which assumed maintenance of the trail in the 1920s, built three shelter cabins, located 20 miles, 30 miles, and 43 miles from Cantwell. Each cabin was built of logs and had the same dimensions (about 14 by 16 feet). A slightly larger log barn to shelter dogs and horses was erected next to each cabin. The 30-mile, or Brushkana Creek Cabin, is the only surviving ARC shelter cabin along the route.

Freighting over the trail was expensive, and the Valdez Creek miners kept pushing for construction of a road. The ARC began upgrading the trail in the 1930s and constructed a wood-truss bridge across Brushkana Creek, about a mile upstream from the 30-mile cabin.

However, by the time the bridge was completed, the ARC had decided to shift the road route to higher ground south of the Nenana River, bypassing the lower section of Brushkana Creek. The Brushkana Creek Bridge was never used…except as building material. Sometime after the bridge was abandoned, an addition to the Brushkana Creek cabin was built with decking salvaged from the bridge. The bridge abutments are still there.

According to a 1936 U.S. Geological Survey report, 30 miles of road were completed by the mid 1930s. The road link to Valdez Creek would not be completed, though, until the Denali Highway was constructed in the 1950s.

The Brushkana Creek cabin (with metal roof) is still in fair condition, although the addition's sod-roof is starting to cave in. The barn is long gone. BLM has boarded up the cabin due to vandalism and unauthorized alterations.

Sitting on public land, the cabin can be easily reached via the three-mile-long Brushkana Creek Trail which starts at the Brushkana Campgound. It's a lovely trail, but when we hiked it in July we saw plenty of moose and bear sign. So if you go, take along bear protection.

Sources:

- *An Historical Resource Study of the Valdez Creek Mining District, Alaska*. Peter F. Dessauer & David W. Harvey. U. S. Bureau of Land Management. 1977
- Correspondence with John Jangala, archeologist with the U.S. Bureau of Land Management. 2013
- *The Broad Pass Region, Alaska- Bulletin 608*. Fred Moffit & Joseph R. Pogue. U. S. Geological Survey. 1915
- "The Valdez Creek Mining District, Alaska in 1936 - Bulletin 897-B." Ralph Tuck. in *Mineral Resources of Alaska*. U. S. Geological Survey. 1936

Denali National Park and Preserve - Toklat River East Fork

Murie Cabin in 1995

# The East Fork Cabin - Adolf Murie's base camp for pioneering wolf studies

As early as 1922, rangers erected a tent near the confluence of the East Fork of the Toklat River and Coal Creek (43 miles from park headquarters) for shelter during winter patrols of Mount McKinley National Park. In 1928 the Alaska Road Commission (ARC), which was building a road through the park, constructed a shelter cabin there.

The "East Fork" cabin became part of a construction camp providing support for constructing a bridge across the East Fork and the section of road over Polychrome Pass. Photos of the camp show about 10 tents spread out below the cabin. After the road was completed, rangers used the cabin for shelter during their patrols.

According to National Register of Historic Places documents, the one-room 14-foot by 16-foot cabin is constructed of peeled logs sawn flat on three sides. The ends of the logs are squared notched. A gable roof extends beyond the cabin front, forming a porch, and there is a small storage platform under the eaves to the left of the front door.

The cabin was originally roofed with rolled roofing, which has been replaced with wood shakes. The rear wall has a small window, and there is a larger double window in the south wall. Both windows were originally multi-pane, but have been upgraded with single-pane windows.

When the cabin is not occupied, the windows are protected with bear-proof shutters (with nails protruding outward to discourage bruins) and a removable bear-proof door.

The cabin has been occupied by many park employees in its 80-plus years but the most well-known resident was Adolf Murie, renowned wildlife biologist and wolf expert. Adolf (1899-1974) first came to Denali in 1922 as the assistant to his older half-brother Olaus Murie, who was studying caribou for the U.S. Biological Survey.

During parts of their "off" seasons, the brothers rented a cabin in Fairbanks. While there they became acquainted with Margaret Thomas and her half-sister, Louise Gillette. Olaus married Margaret in 1924, and Adolf and Louise were married in 1932.

After the 1923 field season Adolf returned to the Lower 48 to complete his education, eventually receiving his Ph.D from the University of Michigan in 1929. He was hired by the newly formed Wildlife Division of the National Park Service in 1934 and was sent back to Mount McKinley National Park in 1939 to study the relationship between wolves and Dall sheep.

During the 1939 field season Adolf worked out of the Igloo Creek patrol cabin at 33 Mile of the park road with two assistants. In his book, The Wolves of Mt. McKinley, he wrote that he hiked about 1,700 miles that summer.

The next summer Adolf (along with his wife, 4-year-old daughter and 1-year-old son) moved into the East Fork cabin. Adolf conducted his wildlife studies solo that year, while Louise and children stayed at the cabin. Adolf wrote of arriving home one evening to discover that Louise, brandishing a stove poker, had been forced to chase a grizzly away from the cabin that day.

Adolf's pioneering wolf study (published in 1944) forever changed how people viewed wolves. He depicted wolves as complex creatures with unique individual personalities and strong family ties. He even named the wolves he studied. Adolf also demonstrated the inter-dependent and generally beneficial relationship between predator and prey.

He later worked full-time at Mount McKinley National Park, and according to the book, *Snapshots from the Past; a roadside history of Denali National Park and Preserve*, spent several full years and over 25 summers" at Denali. Eight of those summers were spent at what is now called the Murie cabin.

Sources:

- "Adolph Murie: Denali's wilderness conscience." Linda Franklin. Master's thesis, University of Alaska Fairbanks. 2004
- *Crown Jewel of the North: An Administrative History of Denali National Park and Preserve, Volume 1.* Frank Norris. National Park Service. 2006
- "Patrol Cabins – Mt. McKinley National Park, National Register of Historic Places Inventory-Nomination Form." National Park Service. 1986
- *Snapshots from the Past, a Roadside history of Denali National Park and Preserve.* Jane Bryant. Center for Resources, Science and Learning, Denali National Park and Preserve. 2011
- *The Wolves of Mt. McKinley*. Adolf Murie. National Park Service. 1944

Quigley cabin in 1995

## Kantishna's Fannie Quigley, a larger-than-life frontier woman

Fannie Quigley was a larger-than-life Alaskan whose story has probably been embellished over the years. A 1990 *Alaska Magazine* article related that Fannie "was quick on the trigger, she could wrestle a bear, she could outsmart a wolf, and she could outdrink and outcuss just about any man in the north."

Undoubtedly overstated, but what isn't exaggerated is that she was an independent spirit in the days when women were supposed to be meek and dependent on men.

Fannie's maiden name was Francis Sedlacek, and she was born in 1871 on a Nebraska homestead to Bohemian immigrants. (Bohemia is now part of the Czech Republic.)

Homesteading the Nebraska prairie was difficult, and Fannie left home when she was 16. She spoke little English growing up, and acquired her "colorful" version of the language from salty railroad workers as she worked her way west, probably waiting on tables and cooking in railroad camps.

She just kept moving west, and in 1899 joined the Klondike gold rush. Fannie ended up in Dawson City, where some stories relate she worked as a dance hall girl. However, with her experience cooking for construction crews, she realized her ticket to possible fortune was not through a dollar-a-dance with lonesome miners, but through the stomachs of hungry stampeders.

Miners on the creeks often had no time or inclination to cook, and were quite willing to pay for a hot meal. Fannie began following the stampeders to new diggings, pulling a sled loaded with tent, Yukon stove and provisions. Arriving at a new camp she would set up her tent, post a sign announcing, "Meals for Sale" and open for business. When activity on one creek died down she would move on. From this business model she earned the handle, "Fannie the Hike."

In 1901 she married Angus McKenzie. The marriage was not to last though, and in 1903 Fannie took off again — alone — for the next rumored strike, 800 miles away in Rampart. According to Jane Haigh's book, *Searching for Fannie Quigley,* her marriage was probably never legally dissolved.

Fannie quickly passed through Rampart and on to the new gold camp at Fairbanks. Then, in 1905, came word of a gold strike in the Kantishna region and Fannie was off again.

After arriving in Kantishna (then called Eureka), for a time she operated a roadhouse called Mother McKenzie's. However, the lure of prospecting had always been strong in Fannie. She staked her first claim in the Kantishna area in 1907, and ended up staking scores of additional claims.

She also staked out a different sort of claim — on Kantishna miner Joe Quigley. By 1907 she and Joe were living together. Many early accounts of Fannie's life, not wishing to offend cultural norms, stated that she and Joe were married in 1906, but in reality they were not married until 1918. (It's possible she did not marry Joe until after her first husband had died.)

In 1930 Joe had a life-threatening accident which ended his mining career. He began spending increasing amounts of time away from Kantishna, and in 1937 the two divorced. Joe eventually moved Outside, but Fannie refused to leave Kantishna.

Earlier that same year the Quigleys sold their claims on the ridge between Friday and Eureka creeks above Kantishna to the Red Top Mining Company (RTMC). It was the RTMC that built the wood-frame home shown in the drawing, either in 1938 or 1939. Located just north of Friday Creek in Kantishna, this is where Fannie moved sometime after 1939, and where she lived until her death in 1944. She is buried in the Birch Hill Cemetery in Fairbanks.

Sources:

- "Fannie Quigley, Frontierswoman," Grant H. Pearson. in *Alaska Sportsman.* August 1947, Vol. 13, No. 08
- "Fannie the Hike." Jo Anne Wold, in *Alaska Magazine.* October 1990, Vol. 56, No. 10
- *Searching for Fannie Quigley*. Jane G. Haigh. Ohio University Press. 2007
- *Snapshots from the Past, a Roadside history of Denali National Park and Preserve*. Jane Bryant. Center for Resources, Science and Learning, Denali National Park and Preserve. 2011

Bucyrus 20-B steam shovel at Usibelli Coal Mine in 2014

## Emil Usibelli and the early years of Usibelli Coal Mine

In 1907, at the age of 14, Emil Usibelli emigrated from Italy to the United States. Settling in Washington state, he worked a variety of jobs, doing stints as a miner, logger, and foundry worker before buying a coal distribution business.

With economic hardships brought on by the Great Depression, Usibelli moved to Alaska in 1935 to start afresh, hiring on as a coal miner at the Evan Jones mine just outside Sutton, about 15 miles northwest of Palmer.

A year later he moved to Interior Alaska, working at "Cap" Lathrop's Healy River Coal Corporation mine at Suntrana, just east of Healy. Laid-off due to a work-related injury, he fell back on his other work skills and established a logging operation supplying timbers to the coal mines.

Between 1940 and 1941 the United States built military installations at Kodiak, Unalaska, Anchorage and Fairbanks, and this military presence greatly increased Alaska's market for coal. During the early years of World War II the Healy River Coal Corporation supplied most of the coal used in Fairbanks by Ladd Field (now called Fort Wainwright) and the civilian population, but was hard-pressed to keep up with the increasing demand.

The book, *Mining the Burning Hills, A History of Suntrana Coal Mine and Townsite,* states that the Federal Coal Commission began looking for additional operators to increase Alaska's coal production. Emil landed a federal contract to explore for coal east of Suntrana. In 1943 he and his friend, T. E. Thad Sanford, obtained a lease on coal lands just upstream from Suntrana, and signed a one year contract to supply Ladd Field with 10,000 tons of coal.

Coal mines in Alaska up until then had been underground operations. Not having the deep pockets necessary develop an underground mine, Emil and Thad began simply—using a McCormick-Deering TD-40 tractor to scrape overburden off surface seams and then pushing the coal into the bed of a truck.

Their methods were primitive but successful. They met their contractual obligations, and from then on gradually expanded and improved the operation. Emil eventually did some underground mining, but concentrated on strip mining since it was safer and more efficient.

The steam shovel shown in the drawing was used during the early years of the mine. According to the "Steam Shovel Registry," it is a Bucyrus model 20-B, weighing 20 tons and having a ¾ cubic yard bucket.

Promotional literature called it a "universal" excavator, since it could be converted from a basic shovel to a dragline, crane, or clamshell shovel with minimal alterations. Retired many years ago, it now sits outside the company's office near Healy.

In 1945 Emil, who handled mine operations, began experimenting with hydraulic stripping (removing overburden with high-pressure jets of water). The sandstone capping the coal seams was too solid to simply be worked hydraulically and had to be drilled and blasted before being washed away. Emil eventually gave the process up and went back to mechanical stripping.

However, during the time he did use hydraulicking his workers make a little extra pocket money. Emil set up sluice boxes to catch the small amount of gold washed out with the overburden, and his workers were allowed to keep whatever gold they recovered.

In 1948 he bought his partner out, and during the 1950s output from the mine surpassed that of his competitors. In 1961 he bought out his main rival, Suntrana Coal Mine (successor to Lathrop's Healy River Coal Company).

Emil was killed in a mine accident on March 24, 1964. His son, Joe, took over management of Usibelli Coal Mine, and he in turn was succeeded by his son, Joe Usibelli, Jr.. The mine is still in operation, managed by the same family for 70 years. It employs about 140 people, and provides coal not only to local utilities, but ships it abroad to customers in Asia and South America.

Sources:

- Conversations with Bill Brophy, Usibelli Coal Mine, Inc. general manager. 2015
- "Emil Usibelli (1893-1964)." Charles Green & Becki Phipps. On Alaska Mining Hall of Fame Foundation website. 2000
- *Mining the Burning Hills: A History of Suntrana Coal Mine and Townsite.* Rolfe G. Buzzell. Alaska Office of History and Archaeology. 1994
- "Steam Shovel Registry" website. Information provided by H. Keith Walters.
- "The Usibelli Story." On Usibelli Coal Mine website, 2015
- "Usibelli Coal Mine celebrating 60 years in Alaska." Christy Caballero. in *Alaska Business Monthly.* 11-2003

Annie Cragg Farthing grave at Nenana Native cemetery in 2012

## Nenana Native Cemetery is a peaceful place to visit

On the south slope of Toghot-thele Hill (pronounced tog-hot-teelee), across the Tanana River from Nenana, sits the Nenana Native Cemetery. It is a wonderfully peaceful place, shaded by aspen, cottonwood, birch and spruce trees. We visited it several years ago in late June and spotted lady's slipper (also called moccasin flower) blossoms profusely covered much of the hillside.

The cemetery is approximately one mile east of the Parks Highway at the end of a gravel road that winds up the hill. There is no overarching design to the site. Most of the graves are in small hollows or on the hill's gentler slopes. Narrow footpaths wind up and down the hillside linking the burial areas. Many of the graves are in family groupings.

A majority of graves are surrounded by fences, which is fairly common for Native burials in many parts of Alaska. Fenced graves are a frequent feature in Alaska's Russian Orthodox cemeteries, but the Orthodox Church did not penetrate into the Tanana River Valley until modern times.

Russians established a trading post at Nulato (an Athabascan village on the west bank of the Yukon River about 300 air miles west of Fairbanks) in 1839, but only traveled beyond that on a seasonal basis. They made periodic trips up the Yukon as far as an Athabascan trading site called Nuklukayet at the confluence of the Yukon and Tanana rivers, but as far as I know, never ascended the Tanana River.

Examples of grave fences could be found in many parts of Eastern Interior Alaska during the late 1800s though. U.S. Army Lieutenant Frederick Schwatka floated down the Yukon River on a reconnaissance trip for the federal government in 1883 and reported fences around Native graves as far east as Fort Selkirk in Canada. He mentioned a grave fence in the Rampart area similar in appearance to "Western" style fences, but the ones in Canada were merely rough boards bound tightly together with cords. It's probably debatable whether erecting burial fences was "borrowed" from Russian America or reflects an independent indigenous tradition.

Athabascan Indians have occupied the lands around Nenana for generations and a seasonal village was located there before Westerners began exploring the Tanana Valley at the beginning of the 1900s. I'm not sure anyone knows exactly how old the cemetery is, but it probably dates to sometime after 1907, when the Episcopal Church started a mission at the village. Church literature first mentions burials at Nenana in 1911, the year a missionary for the church and an Athabascan child were interred on the hillside.

It appears that the main part of the cemetery was originally just along the high bank above the river. After a 1920 influenza epidemic in Nenana, (when up to a quarter of the village's Native residents died) there were about 40 graves located there. However, when the Alaska Railroad built a bridge across the Tanana River and ran its tracks along the base of Toghotthele Hill in the early 1920s it relocated many of the graves higher on the hill.

One of the surprises at the cemetery is a huge Celtic cross (shown in the drawing) that marks the grave of Annie Cragg Farthing, the first Episcopal missionary at Nenana. Farthing, who served at Anvik and Fairbanks before moving to Nenana, was in charge of the mission for its first four years. She died while nursing one of the mission's boarding students (who also died a few days later). She and her young charge were buried side by side on the hillside overlooking the mission.

The cemetery is still in use. Please be respectful if you visit.

Sources:

- *Modern Foragers: wild resource use in Nenana Village, Alaska, Technical Paper No. 91*. Anne Shinkwin & Martha Case. Alaska Department of Fish and Game. 1984.
- Photograph of Nenana Native cemetery taken by Alaska Engineering Commission in 1922. Cook Inlet Historical Society. Anchorage Museum at Rasmuson Center
- Photographs of Nenana Native cemetery between 1915 and 1920. Frederick B. Drane collection. University of Alaska Fairbanks Archives
- *Report of a Military Reconnaissance in Alaska made in 1883*. Frederick Schwatka. U.S. War Department. 1885
- "The Alaskan missions of the Episcopal Church, A brief sketch, historical and descriptive." Hudson Stuck. Domestic and Foreign Missionary Society of the Protestant Episcopal Church in the United States of America, 1920
- *The Spirit of Missions, an illustrated monthly review of Christian missions, Vol. 76*. Domestic and Foreign Missionary Society. 1911
- *The Upper Tanana Indians*. Robert A. McKennan. Yale University. 1959
- U.S. Bureau of Land Management land records

Parks Highway - Nenana

Nenana railroad depot in 2012

## Railroad dramatically changed Nenana

In March 1914, Congress authorized the construction of a government railroad in the Territory of Alaska. The northern terminus of the railroad would be in Fairbanks, but there were two competing routes from ice-free ports at tidewater to the Interior. There was an "eastern" route starting at Valdez or Cordova on Prince William Sound, and a "western" route, starting at Seward or Portage Bay on the Kenai Peninsula.

The future of the Athabascan village of Toghotthele, located near the confluence of the Nenana and Tanana Rivers, was unequivocally affected when President Wilson chose the western route. His decision was influenced in part by national sentiment against J. P. Morgan and the Guggenheim family, whose Alaska Syndicate owned the Copper River and Northwestern Railroad that ran between Cordova and Kennicott.

The western route followed the right of way of the bankrupt Alaska Northern Railroad north from Seward to Turnagain Arm, and then struck out across the Matanuska-Susitna Valley, crossing the Alaska Range at Broad Pass, and heading north to Fairbanks. The proposed railroad crossed the Tanana River at Toghottele (now named Nenana).

The book, *Railroad in the Clouds: the Alaska Railroad in the Age of Steam,* records that the Alaska Engineering Commission (AEC—the government entity formed to oversee the railroad's construction) began work in 1915 at Ship Creek in the newly formed town of Anchorage. By 1916, 60 miles of new track had been laid, 100 miles of roadbed graded and 230 miles of right of way cleared.

Some histories claim that the Alaska Railroad's tracks reached Nenana by 1922, but this is not completely accurate. While the rail link between Anchorage and Nenana was completed in 1922, the AEC had decided to have crews work simultaneously from the south and north. Anchorage was the southern construction headquarters, and Nenana was chosen as the northern headquarters.

Beginning in 1915, the AEC built a sizable construction compound in Nenana, including offices, dormitories, power plant, machine shop, warehouses and hospital. (All of these structures are now gone.) A white man's community sprang up around the railroad yard, and Nenana's population quickly doubled. By this time, Fairbanks's sister city of Chena (at the mouth of the Chena River) was dying, and many of that community's buildings were relocated to the new railroad town at Nenana.

So construction crews worked south from Nenana and north from Anchorage, and in February 1922 the gap between the southern and northern segments was closed with the completion of the Riley Creek Bridge (still in use) just outside the entrance to Denali National Park.

A bridge across the Tanana River still needed to be constructed, but that did not stop rail traffic from reaching Fairbanks. The AEC had acquired the bankrupt Tanana Valley Railroad in 1917, and in 1919 it extended tracks south to the north shore of the Tanana River. Until the Mears railroad bridge across the Tanana was completed in 1923, passengers and freight were ferried across the river when it was free of ice, and during the winter, temporary tracks were laid across the frozen Tanana River.

With the completion of the railroad as far as Nenana, a depot was needed. A single story station with passenger waiting room and freight storage room (similar to the historic depot still standing in Seward) was built in 1922 near the waterfront. In 1937, a second story containing the personal quarters for the railroad agent was added.

According to an article by Pat Durand on the Alaska Rails website, by the 1980s, the depot was no longer being used, and it was transferred to the city of Nenana in 1987. Now the Alaska State Railroad Museum, it is open during the summer free of charge, and is a lovely place to spend a morning or afternoon.

Sources:

- *Railroad in the Clouds: The Alaska Railroad in the age of Steam, 1914-1945.* William H. Wilson. Pruett Publishing. 1977
- "Alaska Engineering Commission (1914-1923)." no author. AlaskaRails.org website. 2004
- "Alaska's Heritage: Chapter 4-11, Railroad Transportation." no author. Alaska History and Cultural Studies website. 2004
- "Nenana Depot History." Patrick Durand. AlaskaRails.org website. 2004
- *Tanana Valley Railroad, the Gold Dust Line.* Nicholas Deely. Denali Designs. 1996

Manley Roadhouse in 1994

## Manley Roadhouse – Serving hospitality since 1903

John Karshner was prospecting for gold when he stumbled across a hot springs in the hills just north of a small Tanana River tributary in 1902. Karshner was originally from Kansas and had a farming background. He looked at the hot springs and saw more potential for profit in selling food to prospectors and miners than in actually mining, so he immediately staked out a homestead north of the stream, which became known as "Hot Springs Slough."

A trading post supplying goods to prospectors in the Tofty and Eureka areas to the north was located about 10 miles to the east, at the confluence of Baker Creek and the Tanana River. However, seeing the advantages of the hot springs site, entrepreneurs soon built a general store on the north side of Hot Springs Slough, eclipsing the Baker Creek operation. The Baker Creek site was located along the route of the Washington-Alaska Military Cable and Telegraph System (WAMCATS) telegraph line and survived for a time as a telegraph station, but except for a small sawmill, otherwise passed into obscurity.

Hot Springs (also called Baker Hot Springs and eventually Manley Hot Springs) was in the ascendant though, and other facilities sprouted up. According to the Manley Roadhouse website, in addition to the store, Sam's Meals and Rooms (which eventually became the Manley Roadhouse) opened in 1903, also on the north side of the slough.

Most of the new town's businesses appear to have been clustered along the base of the hills on the north bank of the slough, rather than on the flatter ground to the south. This was in part because of the Martin Sabin homestead, which occupied about 150 acres on the south side of the slough where the town airport is now. I think it was also because of a military withdrawal on slough's south bank made to support the WAMCATS telegraph line. When the landlines were replaced by wireless telegraphy (radio) most of the telegraph stations closed. Consequently, the military withdrawal at Hot Springs was abandoned, and business began moving across the slough.

In a biography of Stanley Dayo, a long-time Manley resident, he states that the Manley Roadhouse was moved across the slough to its present location in 1925. Late January and early February of 1925 was also when the serum run from Nenana to Nome occurred, during which 20 mushers relayed diphtheria anti-toxin to combat an outbreak of the deadly disease.

The book, *The Cruelest Miles: The Heroic Story of Dogs and Men in a Race Against an Epidemic*, relates the story of Edgar Kalland, an Athabascan musher who carried the serum from Tolovana to Manley, a distance of 32 miles. The temperature during his run was about 55 degrees below zero (F) and one newspaper article reported that upon arriving at the Manley roadhouse, Kalland's mittens were frozen to the sled's handle bar. The roadhouse proprietor reportedly poured boiling water over the handle bar to free Kalland's mittens. (I'm assuming the roadhouse had not been moved before the serum run took place.)

The roadhouse has gone through a succession of owners, but its basic appearance has changed little over the years. The front portion of the establishment, a 2-½ story wood-frame structure with a gable roof, looks pretty much the same as it did when moved across the slough. It is very typical of commercial buildings built during the early 1900s.

The rear section of the building has changed gradually during the years — morphing from a small one-story addition (with additional additions tacked on, Alaska-style) to the present two-story structure. The roadhouse is still operating, serving Alaskan hospitality to locals and visitors year-round.

Sources:

- *An archeological reconnaissance of Manley and Hutlinana Hot Springs, central interior Alaska.* Robert Sattler. University of Alaska Museum. 1986
- "Manley Hot Springs history." John Robert Dart. from Dart Agriculture and Mining website. 2010
- "Manley Roadhouse history." from Manley Roadhouse website. 2009
- *Prospecting and Mining Activity in the Rampart, Manley Hot Springs and Fort Gibbon Mining Districts of Alaska, 1894 to the Present Era.* Rosalie L'Ecuyer. Bureau of Land Management. 1997
- *Stanley Dayo, Manley Hot Springs.* Yvonne Yarber & Curt Madison. Yukon Kuskokwim School District. 1984
- *The Cruelest Miles: The Heroic Story of Dogs and Men in a Race Against an Epidemic.* Gay Salisbury. W.W. Norton. 2003
- U.S. Bureau of Land Management records

Steese Highway - Fairbanks Creek Road

Gilmore McCarty mill in the 1990s

## Old Gilmore/McCarty stamp mill near Fairbanks may soon disappear

Fairbanks Creek, 20 miles northeast of town, was one of the most productive gold producing areas around Fairbanks. Genevieve Parker Metcalfe, who was the first woman graduate of the Alaska School of Mines (now the University of Alaska), lived along Fairbanks Creek from 1914 to 1921.

She noted that several different types of gold mining took place while she lived there. The Alaska Mining Hall of Fame quotes her as saying, "At the head of the creek the McCartys and, just below them, Tom Gilmore, tunneled hard rock. His ore was processed by a stamp mill. Well below, a very small dredge was owned and operated by an English company. Next came the Parker's open-cut scraper mine at the mouth of Crane Gulch. At the lower end of the creek, underground mines were needed to reach gold bearing gravel lying under deep gravel and muck."

Tom Gilmore, whom Genevieve mentioned, was Felix Pedro's partner. He was one of the many "gumboot" miners (the sourdough term for placer miners) who after chasing alluvial gold for years, decided to trace it to its source and try his hand at lode, or hard-rock mining.

He had a lode mine and stamp mill at No. 13 above Discovery (the 13th claim upstream from the discovery claim). Lew McCarty, along with his sons Lawrence and Bill, tunneled at No. 16 above Discovery, about as far up Fairbanks Creek as you can go.

Stamp mills are necessities in lode mining, crushing ore so minerals can be extracted. They accomplish this by pounding the ore with heavy vertical pistons, or stamps, which are raised and then allowed to fall.

The Citizens Mill on Garden Island (near downtown) was the first stamp mill in the Fairbanks area, opening on Feb. 24, 1909. The day was so momentous that the mayor declared it a holiday. The town of Chena, not to be outdone, soon built its own mill.

The drawback to these mills was that miners had to freight ore to them. As lode mining developed, many owners built stamp mills next to their mines, eventually putting the Citizens and Chena mills out of business. At the peak of lode mining, there were about 10 stamp mills operating in the Fairbanks area.

The Gilmore/McCarty Mill (shown in the drawing) was built by Gilmore, and used by himself and the McCartys to process their ore. Eventually the McCarty's purchased the mill. The three story wood-frame structure is built on the side of a hill and has cascading shed roofs, typical of many other stamp mills. I'm not sure what sort of sheathing and roofing the building had originally, but in later years it was covered with tarpaper held in place with furring strips.

Much of the building's machinery is gone, but it still houses two stamps. According to a 1941 report by the College of Mines, each stamp weighs 1,600 pounds and when in operation the stamps could strike 72 times per minute, allowing the mill to process 10 tons of ore each day.

At first, the mill was powered by a coal-fired boiler, but after the mine was acquired by the Fairbanks Exploration Company, electric lines were strung from the company's power plant in Fairbanks.

The mine and mill closed down in 1942 and never re-opened. I've visited several times. When I hiked in last year the mill was choked by surrounding trees, the lowest level's roof had caved in, and the walls were in danger of collapse as well. It looks like this piece of mining history will not survive much longer.

Sources:

- "Genevieve Alice Parker Metcalfe." Vieve Metcalfe, Thomas K. Bundtzen and Earl H. Beistline. Alaska Mining Hall of Fame. 2004
- *Historic Resources in the Fairbanks North Star Borough.* Janet Matheson & F. Bruce Haldeman. Fairbanks North Star Borough. 1981
- "History of Lode Mining, Fairbanks District," parts 1 and 2. Curtis Freeman. in *Alaska Miner.* Vol. 30, nos. 8 (August) & 9 (September) 2002
- "McCarty Mine, Fairbanks District." no author. Mineral and Locality Database, MinDat.org. 2011
- *The McCarty Mine, Fairbanks District, Alaska.* Henry R. Joesting. Department of Mines, Alaska College of Mines. 1941

Steese Highway - Fairbanks Creek Road

Nordale Adit headframe in 2011

## Homestake Mine's Nordale Adit is a remnant of area's lode mining history

Before the development of Fort Knox gold mine northeast of Fairbanks, it's likely that many people had only heard about the Fairbanks area's placer gold production.

The early drift mines and later dredges that tore hundreds of millions of dollars worth of gold from the frozen gravels of streams such as Cleary, Fairbanks, Ester and Engineer creeks received most of the press, but the hills above the streams also supported hard rock mines. The gold-bearing quartz veins in the area were not very large and could never be classified as bonanzas, but they did support a few dozen mines. The remains of some of these mines can still be seen on Ester Dome and in the Cleary Creek drainage.

All placer gold begins as lode gold embedded in rock. When gold-bearing rock such as quartz is exposed, it eventually erodes, freeing at least some of the gold. The gold may then work its way downslope and end up in placer deposits.

Soon after placer gold is discovered in an area, prospectors invariably begin looking for the "mother lodes." Sure enough, according to the U.S. Bureau of Mines publication, *Gold-Lode Deposits, Fairbanks Mining District,* the first gold-quartz claim in the Fairbanks area was staked in 1903, about a year after placer gold was discovered by Felix Pedro.

Five years later, in 1908, the Homestake Mining Company located a gold-quartz claim at the head of Wolf Creek, about 20 miles northeast of Fairbanks. The drawing is of a headframe at one of the mine adits, just up the draw from the company's primary adit at the main mine building. (Adits are the horizontal or nearly horizontal entrances to mines.)

The headframe was used to hoist ore buckets out of the mine. Across the road from the headframe is a building that probably housed the hoist's engine.

This adit is now called the "Nordale Adit," (named for Anton J. Nordale, Fairbanks hotel owner and a principal in the Homestake Mining Company.)

U.S. Geological Survey documents record that between 1908 and 1938, miners excavated more than 800 feet of southerly tunnel, and another 1,500 feet of drifts (tunnels that followed the mineralization) to the east and west. During that same period about 2,900 ounces of gold was taken from the mine. (Much of that gold ore was processed at the McCarty stamp mill, about two miles away on the other side of the ridge.) During World War II, gold mining was considered a non-essential wartime activity, and all gold production in the United States was halted in 1942. The Nordale Adit was closed down, just as every other gold mine was.

Post-war production costs, coupled with the expenses of rehabilitating a closed mine, prevented the re-opening of the Nordale Adit until 1982. The mine then operated until 1986 when the adit's portal collapsed, sealing off the mine.

Numerous other old diggings are located in the immediate area. Old U.S. Geological Survey maps show at least a half dozen old mine sites within a mile of the Nordale Adit. Standing on the edge of the road, mere yards from the headframe, you can look down Wolf Creek gulch and see the ruins of the Homestake Mine's main building about 300 feet below.

The friend who tipped me off about the Nordale Adit warned me that there are open shafts in the area, so anyone who goes poking around should be very careful. The headframe is located on state land but there is private property nearby. Please be respectful of property rights.

Sources:

- *A Geologic Reconnaissance of the Fairbanks Quadrangle. U.S. Geological Survey Bulletin 525.* L. M. Prindle. U.S. Geological Survey. 1913
- *Gold Lode Deposits, Fairbanks Mining District.* Bruce Thomas. U.S. Bureau of Mines. 1973,
- "Homestake Mine." C.J. Freeman & J.R. Guidetti Schaefer. Alaska Resource Data File, U.S. Geological Survey. 1999
- *Mineralization in the Wolf Creek-Fairbanks Creek Area.* Robert Warfield. U.S. Bureau of Mines. 1970
- *Mineral Resources of Alaska, U.S. Geological Survey Bulletin 662.* Alfred Brooks. U.S. Geological Survey. 1916

Samppi Mine at Ruby Creek in the 1990s

# Samppi Mine near Chatanika typical of old drift mines that dot Interior Alaska

The giant dredges scattered along the creeks around Fairbanks are testament to the decades when dredging dominated local gold production, just as the headframes and mill buildings in the hills are reminders of hard-rock mining.

However, there are few reminders of the drift mines that initially supported Fairbanks and the mining camps surrounding it. The major reason so few of these operations still exist is because the dredges reworked much of the creek bottoms, tearing up any evidence of previous mining activity.

The drawing is of the above ground portion of the Samppi drift mine on Ruby Creek, about two miles south of Chatanika near the old Tanana Valley Railroad right-of-way. Dredges never made it to this area.

Placer miners in the Fairbanks area had to deal with the thick layers of frozen "muck" that covered the gold-bearing gravels. Miners burrowed down to those gravels, and then followed the "paystreak" by digging horizontal tunnels called drifts.

According to the book, *Historic Resources in the Fairbanks North Star Borough*, the initial step was sinking vertical exploratory shafts. (Where I grew up in California, these were called "coyote holes.")

Digging through frozen soil is excruciatingly tedious, so the frozen ground was first thawed with a fire or hot rocks (later with steam points), and the thawed soil excavated. This process was repeated until bedrock was reached. If miners were lucky, they found gold in sufficient quantity to mine. If not, they started over again elsewhere.

If gold was discovered the miners drifted along the paystreak, thawing the ground, excavating the gold-bearing gravel and hauling it to the surface. All this had to be done while the above-ground air temperature was below freezing. Miners foolish enough to excavate in frozen ground during warm weather ran the risk of collapsed tunnels.

The simplest drift mines used hand-cranked windlasses to lift gravel to the surface. Larger operations like the Samppi mine used steam-operated winches and a "gin pole" system. A gin pole is a pole standing to the side of a shaft. (In the case of the Samppi Mine, it was two poles lashed together.) The pole is held in position with guy wires.

Most operations also used three additional cables: a "high line" fastened to the top of the pole on which a "carrier" rode to move the ore bucket; a hoist cable to lift the bucket out of the shaft and pull the carrier up to the gin pole, and a trip cable.

The chain on the front of the ore bucket was looped over the trip cable, and would automatically dump the bucket when the carrier reached the winter dump site. In this way gold-bearing gravel was stockpiled until summer when it could be sluiced out.

The Samppi Mine was operated by Melvin Samppi. I couldn't find any mention of the mine in old issues of the *Fairbanks Daily News-Miner,* but there are ample references to Melvin and his wife, Devina, who were active in Fairbanks during the 1930s and 40s.

The last time I visited the mine there were still three buildings standing: a bunkhouse, the boiler and hoist shack, and an outhouse. (Actually, the boiler house was barely standing — the boiler's stack had collapsed onto the roof, and there was asbestos insulation everywhere.) The gin pole was still standing and the ore bucket (with attached carrier) was sitting in the trees. Ruby Creek runs between the gin pole and the mine shaft, and just upstream was a containment dam to stockpile water for sluicing.

If you do go out tramping in the hills, always check land ownership before you go. I crossed private property to get to Ruby Creek, but had permission from the property owner.

Also, in most mining areas there is always the danger of abandoned shafts, often concealed by vegetation. Out in the Ruby Creek area I once stepped in what I thought was a small pool between several tussocks and dropped up to my armpits into what I assume was an old shaft. The tussocks saved me and I was able to pull myself out. Look before you leap.

Sources:

- "Alaska Mining History and Techniques." No author. National Park Service, no date
- *Historic Resources in the Fairbanks North Star Borough.* Janet Matheson & F. Bruce Haldeman. Fairbanks North Star Borough. 1981
- News articles in the *Fairbanks Daily News-Miner* for the years 1938, 1939, 1940, 1941
- *Placer Deposits of Alaska. U.S. Geological Survey Bulletin 137.* Edward H. Cobb. U.S. Geological Survey. 1973,
- *Tanana Valley Railroad, the Gold Dust Line.* Nicholas Deely. Denali Designs. 1996

Steese Highway - Nome Creek

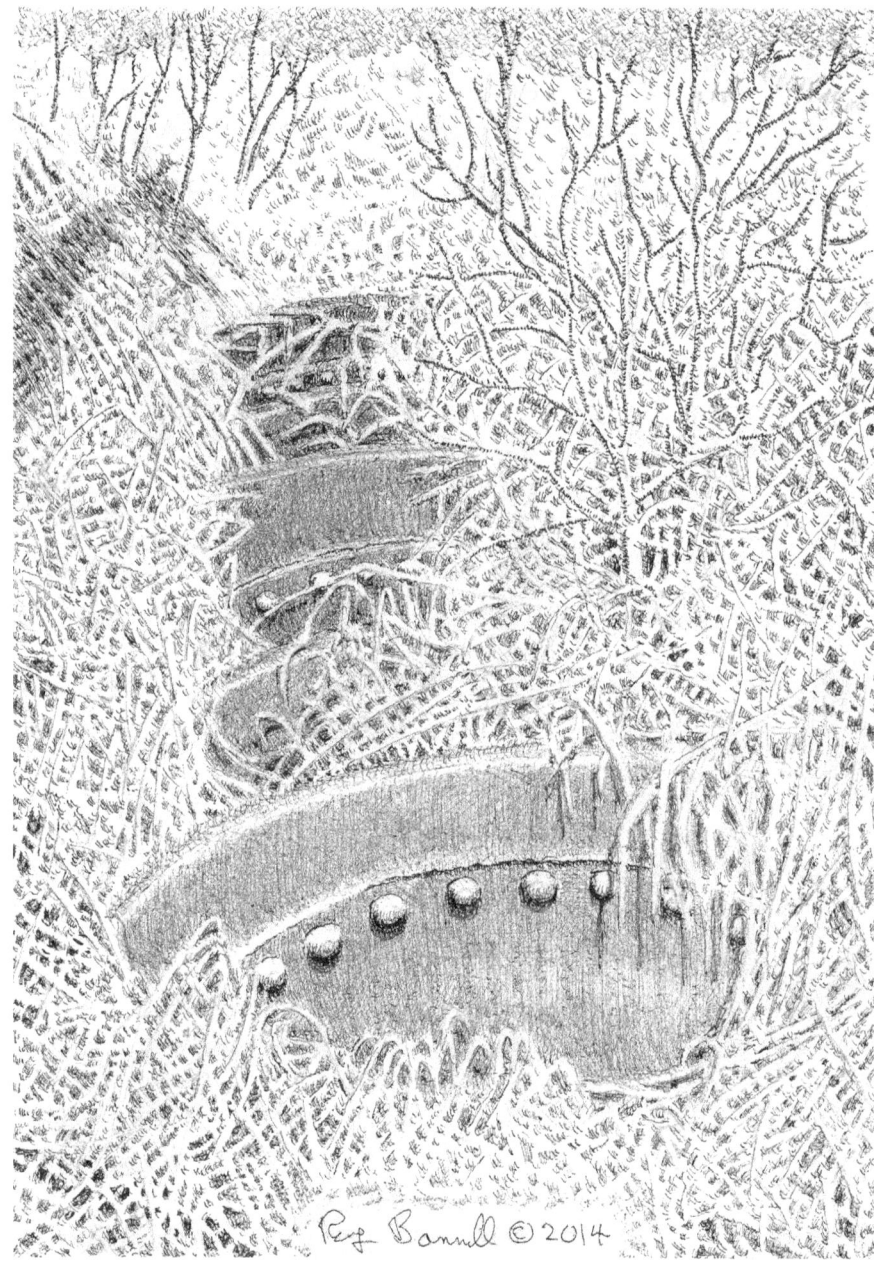
Dredge buckets sinking into muskeg along Nome Creek in 2014

# Mining remnants still visible in Nome Creek Basin

The footprint left by mining on the Nome Creek Basin north of Fairbanks appears minimal at first glance. It's obvious that the creek has been worked, but no buildings remain from the historic mining period and only scattered pieces of mining equipment are left.

However, the paucity of physical evidence belies the fact that two gold dredges once worked the creek's gravels. The dredge buckets shown in the drawing, slowly sinking into the muskeg, are a few of the relics left from one of these dredging operations.

Nome Creek is a 22-mile long tributary of Beaver Creek located in the White Mountains north of Fairbanks. It is within the White Mountains National Recreation Area, managed by the Bureau of Land Management (BLM), and is accessed via the U.S. Creek Road at Mile 57.5 of the Steese Highway. (A section of the Davidson Ditch can also be seen from U.S. Creek Road.)

According to the BLM report, *Beaver Creek National Wild River Cultural Resources Inventory*, the region's original inhabitants were Birch Creek or "Tennuth" Kutchin Athabascans. Tragically, the Birch Creek Kutchin were decimated by a scarlet fever epidemic.

Gold was discovered along Beaver Creek shortly before 1900, but the actual date of discovery is unknown. (When the mining district's first recorder left the country, he took the minutes and books for the district with him).

In 1900 the discovery claim on Nome Creek was staked near the creek's lower end, just across from the mouth of Ophir Creek. During the next decade a few score miners trickled into the area.

That changed in the summer of 1910, with a major discovery along Ophir Creek. Lured by exaggerated tales of diggings richer than the Iditarod, several hundred miners from the Fairbanks vicinity stampeded into the Nome Creek Basin. The U.S. Geological Survey report, *Placer Deposits of Alaska*, states that by the end of 1910 all the ground in the Nome Creek and neighboring basins had been staked.

Extracting gold from the frozen gravels of the creek bottoms was laborious. Most miners earned only meager profits (if they earned a profit at all), and by 1912 the area's population had dwindled to about 25 hardy souls. The gold was still there, but it was beyond the resources of most individuals to economically wrest it from the ground.

In 1925 the Nome Creek Dredging Company was formed, and built a small dredge on Nome Creek in 1926. It was originally powered by a wood-fired steam boiler (a real problem considering the scarcity of timber in the area), but the dredge's owners replaced the boiler with diesel generators in 1930. The dredge operated until 1932 when it was destroyed by fire and never rebuilt.

Seven years later the Deadwood Mining Company moved its dredge about 40 miles from Deadwood Creek near Central to Nome Creek. Photographs from this period show a structure very similar to the Fairbanks Exploration Company dredge now at Chicken.

The Deadwood Mining Company reorganized as the Nome Creek Mining Company and operated its dredge from 1940 to 1942, when gold mining was closed during World War II. The dredge worked again from 1945 to 1947 before permanently shutting down, and then sat rusting in Nome Creek for many years before being dismantled for salvage.

One very visible remnant of the gold dredging era is a two-mile section of Nome Creek called the "Maze." Nome Creek wanders down the center of the valley for most of its course, but through the Maze (located a mile or so below the bridge) the creek zig-zags back-and-forth across the valley floor between tailing piles.

The BLM has improved the roads in the area, built a bridge across Nome Creek, and constructed two campgrounds: Mt. Prindle Campground about two miles above the bridge, and Ophir Creek Campground about 12 miles downstream.

In between is a stretch of Nome Creek open to recreational gold panning (hand-tools only). There is also a put-in at Ophir Creek Campground for boaters floating Beaver Creek.

If you do visit the area, remember that the historical artifacts you see are part of our cultural heritage. Leave them in place for future visitors to find and enjoy.

Sources:

- *Beaver Creek National Wild River Cultural Resources Inventory*. Susan Will. U.S. Bureau of Land Management. 1986
- "Campgrounds rise up from mountains of mining tailings." Jeff Krauss. in *Alaska Frontiers*. U.S. Bureau of Land Management. July/August 1998
- "History of Gold Mining on Nome Creek." Sarah McGowan. U.S. Bureau of Land Management. 2011
- Photos of Deadwood Creek dredge in 1930s. Lawrence Collection. Circle District Historical Society
- *Placer Deposits of Alaska, Geological Survey Bulletin 1374*. Edward H. Cobb. U.S. Geological Survey. 1973
- "Placer Mining in the Yukon-Tanana Region." C. E. Ellsworth & G. L. Parker. in *Mineral Resources of Alaska*. U.S. Geological Survey. 1911

Steese Highway - Sourdough Creek

The "Big House" at Sourdough Creek Camp in 2012

## Remote Sourdough Creek camp offered modern conveniences in 1930s

Sourdough Creek flows south out of the White Mountains and empties into the Chatanika River at about 66 Mile Steese Highway.

Several miles upstream, along Sourdough Creek Road, lies the old Zimmerman/Carlson mining camp. Tony Zimmerman, who also mined on Pedro Creek, developed the site in the early 1930s. (Zimmerman is a well-known Fairbanks name. Birch Hill Cemetery sits on the old Zimmerman homestead.)

Tony mined along Sourdough Creek and constructed the camp, impressive for both its size and refinements, to support his activities. Four buildings remain today: two large 1 1/2 story houses, and two smaller single story cabins. All of the buildings are constructed of notched logs.

Carl J. Carlson, a Fairbanks resident, (his son Karl owned Music Mart) bought the camp from Zimmerman in 1954, and did hydraulic mining along the creek.

Hydraulicking is a method of placer mining where high-pressure jets of water are used to dislodge mineral-bearing material, which is then directed to sluice boxes.

The Carlson family still owns and uses the camp. Carl's granddaughter, Barbara Johnson, told me he apprenticed as a carpenter in Sweden before immigrating to the United States, and worked for the Alaska Railroad as a carpenter before buying the camp.

It was Carl who added white frame porches to all the buildings, plus the beveled eave brackets and other detailing that lend a Craftsman appearance to the camp. The Craftsman, or Arts and Crafts movement, refers to a design philosophy popular during the late 1800s and early 1900s. In Craftsman architecture, some typical exterior details are large porches, gable roofs, wide eaves, and exterior roof supports.

Barbara also told me that she thinks Zimmerman had plans for the camp beyond mining. She remembers an old sign (long gone) along the Steese Highway that announced the "Sourdough Camp Resort."

In addition to the Craftsman styling, the camp's accoutrements set it apart from your typical mining camp. A spring uphill from the camp provided piped running water, and three of the buildings even boasted indoor plumbing. The only building with working plumbing now is the main house (what the Carlsons refer to as the "cook house.") It has a hot water tank with a heat exchanger hooked up to the wood stove, so they even have hot and cold running water.

The building in the drawing is the only structure visible from the road, (the camp is on private property so if you visit the area, please do not trespass.) The Carlsons call it the "big house" and it has a small cribbed basement containing a large wood-burning furnace (now unused), with vents in the floor to evenly distribute the heat. Another of Carl's granddaughters, Janine Thibedeau, said the problem with the furnace in the basement is that the basement floods every spring.

The camp was almost lost in 2004 when the Boundary Fire swept through the area. Fire essentially surrounded the camp, and it was only through the efforts of firefighters to cut a 50- to 100-foot perimeter around the camp that it was saved. Fortunately, the only building that was lost was a garage on the edge of the property.

It really would have been a tragedy if the camp had been destroyed. It is an excellent example of 1930s construction and shows how log construction can be successfully married to other architectural styles. It also proves that advanced plumbing and heating methods could be, and often were incorporated into log houses of this period, sometimes in remote areas.

Sources:

- Conversation with Barbara Johnson and Janine Thibedeau, granddaughters of Carl Carlson
- Fairbanks North Star Borough property records
- "Family Praises Fire Crews,. Mary Beth Smetzer. in *Fairbanks Daily News-Miner.* June 20, 2004
- *Historic Resources in the Fairbanks North Star Borough.* Janet Matheson & Bruce Haldeman. Fairbanks North Star Borough. 1981,

Adams "Leaning Wheel" grader used on Steese Highway, now at Circle District Museum in Central

## Fairbanks-Circle Trail gradually morphed into Steese Highway

Ever since the 1892 discovery of gold along a Yukon River tributary called Birch Creek, prospectors have been tramping the region searching for riches. Miners primarily worked streams such as Mastodon, Miller and Independence Creeks draining northward towards the Yukon, but a few hardy souls crossed Twelvemile Summit (so named because it was 12 miles from early miners' diggings on Birch Creek) to explore the headwaters of the Chatanika River, which drains into the Tanana.

When Judge James Wickersham first visited Fairbanks in the spring of 1903 he mushed southwest through this region from the Yukon River community of Circle. He later wrote in his book, *Old Yukon: Tales, Trails and Trials,* of overnighting in a one-room log roadhouse near the mouth of Faith Creek just south of Twelvemile Summit. The cabin had been constructed in 1901 by Circle stampeders.

A system of trails from Circle to the mines was blazed during the early years of the Circle Mining District, and these became part of the Fairbanks-Circle Trail, a primary route for freighters and mail carriers. Running northeasterly from Fairbanks, the trail followed the Chatanika River, crossed Twelvemile and Eagle summits, ran along

Crooked Creek to Central, and then across lowlands to Circle.

The Alaska Road Commission (ARC) was formed in 1905 and took over the responsibility for the Fairbanks-Circle Trail. By the mid 1910s it had built a rough wagon road from Circle as far south as Miller House (a popular roadhouse) just north of Eagle Summit.

As with many early trails, The Fairbanks-Circle Trail included summer and winter routes. These seasonal alternatives could be found on sections of the trail north of Central and south of Twelvemile Summit.

Some maps show the southern end of the trail wending its way northeast from Fairbanks, skirting the hills south of the Chatanika River before ascending Twelvemile Summit. However, a 1928 ARC map labels this route as a summer trail and indicates that the winter trail lay next to the Chatanika River on its north side. It was this winter route that Judge Wickersham traveled in 1903.

In the early 1920s the ARC began improving the Chatanika end of the trail, installing bridges across streams and constructing shelter cabins and a road along a route above the old winter trail on the north side of the Chatanika River. Most of the work was done in tandem with construction of the Davidson Ditch by the Fairbanks Exploration Company (FE Co.). The initial work, however, was accomplished before the FE Co. began exploration work in the Fairbanks area. By 1926 the road reached the upper limit of the Chatanika River, just below Faith and McManus creeks, where the Davidson Ditch's containment dam was located.

The ARC then extended the road over Twelvemile and Eagle summits, linking up with the Circle-Miller House road, and re-routed portions of the Circle to Central road. (Oscar Bredlie, an early freighter and mail carrier between Fairbanks and Circle, related in an interview with Jane Williams that the Circle to Central road used to be as "crooked as a dog's hind leg.")

The ARC also upgraded the entire road to automobile standards. Bulldozers hadn't been developed yet, and tractor-pulled scrapers and graders accomplished most of the road construction, supported by WW I-era GMC and 1920s Ford Model T trucks. The 1920s-era Adams grader shown in the drawing was used on the road and is now located at the Circle District Museum in Central.

The Fairbanks to Circle road was officially opened in 1928 although freighters utilized the brushed-out right-of-way between Central and Circle before the road was actually completed. Freighters and mail carriers also continued to travel the old "abandoned" winter trail whenever practicable since it cut 12 miles off the distance between Central and Circle.

The road was later named the Steese Highway in honor of General James Steese, former president of the Alaska Road Commission. It used to be billed as the farthest-north highway in the United States (before the Dalton Highway was built), and is still an important year-round connection between Fairbanks and Circle.

Sources:

- Alaska Road Commission map of Steese Highway. Rare Map Collection at University of Alaska Fairbanks Archives. 1928
- *History of Alaskan Operations of United States Smelting, Refining and Mining Company.* John Boswell. University of Alaska. 1979
- *Old Yukon: Tales, Trails, and Trials.* James Wickersham. Washington Law Book Company. 1938
- Oscar Bredlie interview by Jane Williams. Oral History Collection at University of Alaska Fairbanks Archives. 1983
- *Paving Alaska's Trails, the work of the Alaska Road Commission.* Claus-M. Naske. University Press of America. 1986
- Tom Long interview by Harrie Hughes. Oral History Collection at University of Alaska Fairbanks Archives. 1961

The Central Roadhouse in the mid 1980s

# Venerable Central Roadhouse almost made it to 21st century

In the summer of 1896, Josiah Spurr, Frank Schrader and Harold Goodrich floated the Yukon River, investigating mining areas for the U.S. Geological Survey. One of their objectives was the "Birch Creek Diggings" (now called the Circle Mining District) 50 miles southwest of Circle. In Spurr's book, *Through the Yukon Gold Diggings*, he relates that during their Birch Creek side-trip they patronized four roadhouses.

The first was 12-Mile Roadhouse, located where the trail crossed Birch Creek. From there the trail divided, with one branch heading south-southwest to Deadwood Creek (then called Hog'em Gulch) approximately seven miles east of Central. Hog'em Junction Roadhouse was located where Deadwood Creek emptied into Crooked Creek.

The other branch veered west roughly following the current route of the Steese Highway through what we now call Central. Mammoth Junction Roadhouse (later called Miller House) was located on Mammoth Creek just north of Eagle Summit, about 32 miles from 12-Mile roadhouse. Central Roadhouse was situated where the trail from Mammoth Creek crossed Crooked Creek, about midway between Miller House and 12-Mile Roadhouse.

With the 1902 discovery of gold in the hills north of the Chena River, a route linking the Circle-Miller House trail to Fairbanks developed. In Judge James Wickersham's book, *Old Yukon: Tales, Trails and Trials*, he mentioned lunching at Central Roadhouse on his way from Circle to Fairbanks in the spring of 1903.

The Hog'em Junction Roadhouse eventually disappeared, probably after the Alaska Road Commission finished upgrading the Circle-Miller House trail into a wagon road in the early 1910s. Central Roadhouse survived and prospered though, and a small community grew up around it, providing shelter for travelers, and goods and services for miners in the surrounding hills.

Little is known of the roadhouse's earliest owners, but by the 1920s it was owned by Henry "Old Man" Stade. During this period Alf "Riley" Erickson (who eventually took over the roadhouse) began working there. (Erickson was also the Central postmaster from 1925-42.)

After the roadhouse burned down in 1925, Stade and Erickson immediately rebuilt. According to National Register of Historic Places documents, by 1926 they had replaced the original one-story roadhouse with a larger two-story 20-by-52-foot log structure (shown in the drawing). The new roadhouse had a shallow gable roof insulated with dirt and covered with galvanized metal roofing.

The roadhouse, which was situated south of and directly adjacent to the road, originally had a small arctic entry on its northern road-facing side, and a large storage shed tacked on to the south side. There were also numerous outbuildings, including a residence next to the roadhouse, and a barn and several warehouses across the road.

The Steese Highway, completed in 1928, brought more traffic through Central, but reduced the need for overnight lodging. Circle Hot Springs Hotel, opened in 1930, offered better accommodations, and travelers between Fairbanks and Circle often bypassed the roadhouse.

The roadhouse served as a community center for many years, but that wasn't really enough to keep it solvent. In 1948, several months after the owner, Riley Erickson, died, the roadhouse closed and never re-opened. The new owners used the roadhouse building for storage after that, installing garage doors (shown in the drawing) on the east end of the building.

The outbuildings gradually disappeared, but the roadhouse itself survived and was added to the National Register of Historic Places in 1977. Its owners hoped to rehabilitate the structure into a community center and museum, but decades of neglect made the project too expensive. However, when the Circle District Historical Society Museum was constructed about a half mile down the road, many of the roadhouse's furnishings and accoutrements were moved there.

According to Central resident Al Cook, repeated vandalism and trespassing forced the building's owners to raze it in the early 1990s. All that is left is a pile of logs beside the Steese Highway, just east of Crooked Creek.

Sources:

- *Alaska's historic roadhouses*. Michael Smith. Alaska Division of Parks, 1974
- "Central Roadhouse - National Register of Historic Places Inventory-Nomination Form." Jane Williams & Patricia Oakes. National Park Service. 1977
- Conversation with Al Cook, resident of Central. 2015
- Jane Williams interview by Laurel Tyrrel. Oral History Collection at University of Alaska Fairbanks Archives. 1995. Jane was a long-time resident of Central and co-owner of the Central Roadhouse.
- *Old Yukon: Tales, Trails, and Trials*. James Wickersham. Washington Law Book Company. 1938
- Ruth Olson interview by Laurel Tyrrel. Oral History Collection at University of Alaska Fairbanks Archives. 1995. Ruth was a long-time resident of Central.
- *Through the Yukon Gold Diggings, a narrative of personal travel*. Josiah Edward Spurr. Eastern Publishing. 1900.

Old Circle City cabin in the spring of 2014

## Ups and downs of Circle City, the "Paris of the North"

Circle is a small, predominantly Athabascan community at the end of the Steese Highway 160 miles northeast of Fairbanks. Located on the Yukon River's south bank, it began life in 1894 as the supply center for the Circle Mining District 50 miles to the southeast, and as a winter haven for miners frozen out of their diggings.

The cabin in the drawing, dating from Circle's early days, is located near the town cemetery. It is constructed of squared spruce logs with dove-tailed corners (a traditional Scandinavian technique) and has a galvanized metal roof. It was owned by Circle homesteader, Henry Appel, who willed the building to the Pioneers of Alaska when he died.

According to Melody Webb's book, *Yukon, the last frontier*, gold was discovered along Birch Creek in 1892, but mining did not begin until the next year. In the spring of 1893 the discoverers, Sergei Cherosky and Pitka Pavaloff, returned to their claims after obtaining grubstakes from Leroy "Jack" McQuesten, an agent for the Alaska Commercial Company (ACC) at the gold camp of Fortymile. They were trailed by miners following rumors of a new strike.

The region's creeks proved rich, but during the district's early years miners didn't overwinter on their claims. The winter of 1893-94 most lived at a site called "Fish Camp," upriver from Circle's present location.

Flooding the next spring forced the camp's move downstream to a high riverbank on the edge of the Yukon Flats. A townsite was laid out and named Circle City. (Founders erroneously believed they were north of the Arctic Circle when they were actually about 50 miles to the south.)

Strung out along the riverbank, Circle quickly developed into a settlement of 300-400 log cabins. It also boasted several stores (including McQuesten's ACC store), a hospital, Episcopal church, school, opera house (described by some as essentially a two-story dance hall), numerous dance halls and saloons, and even a newspaper. It claimed to be the largest log cabin city in the world.

Some residents called it the "Paris of the North." James Wickersham, in his book, *Old Yukon: Tales, Trails and Trials*, wrote that in Circle's heyday "its inhabitants were a cosmopolitan lot. Bearded and roughly dressed miners from the creeks, gamblers, actresses, prospectors, preachers, merchants, prostitutes, dog-mushers, hunters, dance-hall fairies, and dogs – a frontier gathering from every land, drawn together by the lure of a mining camp stampede." Athabascan Indians also lived on the edge of town and mingled with Circle's other residents.

A few writers were less enthusiastic. Josiah Spurr, who visited Circle in the summer of 1896 with a U.S. Geological Survey expedition, described it as simply, "a settlement of log huts dignified by the name of Circle City."

According to Spurr's account, Circle's population was about 700 people, but only during winter. In summer the population shrank to a few hundred as miners returned to their claims. In any event, Circle's glory days ended in the fall of 1896 when word of the Klondike gold strike filtered down the Yukon River. Most miners abandoned their claims to join the stampede to Dawson City. By the spring of 1897 not more than 50 people, mostly women and children, remained in Circle.

The town recovered when disgruntled miners, unhappy with Canadian regulations and the lack of stakeable ground, began returning in the fall of 1898. By 1899 Circle's population had rebounded to its pre-Klondike numbers, but the 1900 Nome gold rush once again emptied the town of most miners. Later stampedes lured others away.

The miners who stayed gradually adopted new mining techniques and fewer sought winter refuge in Circle. The town never again approached the population it had during its pre-1900 glory days. It survived as a regional supply center until completion of the Steese Highway in 1928 allowed miners to ship supplies out of Fairbanks.

Most of the town's old buildings have been destroyed. Some were razed by fires, others have been torn down (with building materials either re-used or burned as fuel), and many were lost to river bank erosion

The only surviving buildings from Circle's early days are a few cabins scattered around town and the Washington Alaska Military Cable and Telegraph System wireless radio station. Circle now has just two small stores and most residents live a subsistence lifestyle.

Sources:

- Conversation with Earla Hutchinson, co-owner of HC Company Store in Circle
- *Gold Placers of the Circle District, Alaska—Past, Present, and Future.* Warren Yeend. U.S. Geological Survey. 1991
- *Old Yukon: Tales, Trails, and Trials.* James Wickersham. Washington Law Book Company. 1938
- *Yukon, The Last Frontier: A History of the Yukon Basin of Canada and Alaska.* Melody Webb. University of New Mexico Press. 1985
- *Through the Yukon Gold Diggings, a narrative of personal travel.* Josiah Edward Spurr. Eastern Publishing. 1900.

Nels Rasmussen house in Circle in 2014

## Circle's Rasmussen House a freighting pioneer's legacy

Circle City, with a pre-1900 population of about 800 people, saw its population drop to a few hundred after the turn of the century. The town was established in 1894 as a supply center and winter haven for miners from the Circle Mining District 50 miles to the southeast. However, many of the miners moved on to other gold strikes, and those that stayed increasingly spent winters on their claims.

No longer a winter haven for miners, Circle survived as a supply center. Several companies, including the Alaska Commercial Company, operated stores and had warehouses at Circle, and the town was a regular stop for steamboats.

The first trails from Circle to the mines were rough — simple blazed paths across the rolling hills and muskeg between the Yukon River and mountains. Josiah Spurr, who toured the mining regions along the Yukon for the U.S. Geological Survey, tramped the trails of the Circle Mining District in the summer of 1896. He slogged along the muddy byways between Circle and the mines, sometimes along poorly blazed paths that disappeared into the muskeg, and always through clouds of mosquitoes. In his book, *Through the Yukon Gold Diggings*, Spurr wrote of the "Bloodcurdling stories told of the torments of some that had dared to try [the trail] and how strong men had sat down on the trail to sob, quite unable to withstand the pest."

One of the early freighters along the route was Nels Rasmussen. Nels emigrated from Denmark to the U.S. in 1896 and eventually settled at Circle.

His occupation in the 1900 U.S. Census was listed as logger and at one time he owned a small sawmill in the Circle area. (A typical Alaskan entrepreneur, he also owned a saloon in Circle, operated the town's first telephone company, and had mining claims at Woodchopper Creek to the southeast.)

Nels began freighting with sure-footed mules, but as trails improved and eventually were upgraded to roads, he switched to horses, first in pack trains, and then pulling freight wagons. Nels eventually owned 16 horses, and employed several drivers. To feed those horses he raised oats and grain on a homestead he staked in Circle, and on acreage near Jump Off Roadhouse about 25 miles southeast of town.

In 1901 he married Axinia Cherosky, who was related to Sergei Cherosky and Pitka Pavaloff, the discovers of gold along Birch Creek. Axinia, like Sergei and Pitka, was a descendent of Russian/Athabascan "creoles," (the progeny of Russian men and Native women).

It is interesting to note that creoles had a high social status in Russian America. They were often well-educated and many held positions in the Russian Navy and the Russian-American Company. When the United States purchased Alaska, creoles were offered the opportunity to return to Russia as full Russian citizens. Those that remained unfortunately plummeted to the position of "half-breed," which many Americans considered to be even lower than full-blooded Natives.

Nels and Axinia had eight children, and to house their large brood, Nels built an expansive two-story log house (shown in the drawing) as his Circle homestead in about 1909.

It had a two-story porch on the south end of the house, and a one-story addition on the west side. Early photos show the house surrounded by a picket fence. Located just a few hundred feet from the river, the big house became the de facto social center of town.

According to a 1976 *Fairbanks Daily News-Miner* article, Nels was injured in a woodchopping accident in 1920 from which he never fully recovered. He died the next fall and was buried in the town cemetery. Axinia continued to raise her family in the house, and it is still owned by their descendants.

The house's first-floor windows are level with the ground, and Nels' granddaughter, Mary Warren, told me that just shows how much the structure has settled over the years.

While it may have settled and sagged it is still in relatively good condition. Although the house is now vacant, its first floor windows and doors boarded up to prevent vandalism, Nels' descendants want to keep the property and hopefully fix it up for future generations to enjoy.

Sources:

- Conversation with Mary Warren, granddaughter of Nels and Axinia Rasmussen. 2014
- "Rasmussen House stands as memory." Marjorie J. Hay. in *Fairbanks Daily News-Miner*. March 20, 1976
- *Russian Administration of Alaska and the Status of the Alaska Natives*. Law Library of Congress. U. S. Government Printing Office. 1950
- *Through the Yukon Gold Diggings, a narrative of personal travel*. Josiah Edward Spurr. Eastern Publishing. 1900.
- U.S. Census Records for 1900
- *Yukon Frontiers—Historic Resource Study of the Proposed Yukon-Charley National River*. Melody Webb Grauman. National Park Service. 1977

Barn at Colorado Creek Roadhouse in the fall of 2012

# Colorado Creek Roadhouse welcomed travellers headed to Chena Hot Springs

Chena hot Springs Road is paved its entire length. If you drive the 60 miles from Fairbanks to Chena Hot Springs, the trip only takes an hour or so. However, during the first few decades of the 20th century, 20-25 miles a day was about the most a person could travel overland through rural Alaska, and a trip to the springs normally took several days.

For years the quickest and most reliable way to reach the springs was along a winter trail blazed on the north side of the river. Old maps show the trail running from Fairbanks south of the present location of Chena Hot Springs Road (CHSR) until reaching Pleasant Valley, about 27 miles from town. From there it ran along the base of the hills north of CHSR until reaching the springs.

To serve travelers headed to and from the hot springs, three roadhouses were built along the route: Little Chena Roadhouse (at about mile 14 CHSR), Colorado Creek Roadhouse (near mile 32) and Gregg's Roadhouse (at mile 48).

Little Chena Roadhouse has long since disappeared. The remains of Gregg's Roadhouse are reportedly still standing but I have not visited them. I have been to Colorado Creek Roadhouse, though.

The roadhouse at Colorado Creek is located about one mile north of 31 Mile CHSR, just east of a usually shallow ford across Colorado Creek. (That ford wasn't so shallow when I hiked out there, though. Most years you can easily wade across, but I had to slog across the creek through frigid thigh-high water.)

According to the 1985 book, *Historic Resources of the Fairbanks North Star Borough*, Colorado Creek Roadhouse was in operation by 1908. I haven't been able to establish who built the roadhouse, but its proprietors in the 1920s were Alexander Johnston and his wife.

The field notes for the Johnsons' 1928 homestead survey shows that they had quite an operation, with a large residence/roadhouse building, two barns (including the one shown in the drawing), a storage building, greenhouse, root cellar, and chicken coop. All of the buildings were constructed of logs. The Johnsons also had six fenced acres under cultivation.

Chena Hot Springs Road was extended as far as Pleasant Valley by the 1950s, and in the 1960s eventually reached the springs. Don Hymer, who helped stake the road right-of-way during the winter of 1959-60 told me Colorado Creek Roadhouse was abandoned when his survey crew used it as a base camp that winter.

By 1985 there were four buildings left: the roadhouse, a two-story barn, a small log cabin, and an outhouse. Now everything is in ruins. The walls of the roadhouse have collapsed (although the roof is still more-or-less intact) and the roof of the barn has collapsed (although the walls are more-or-less intact). The small cabin is a pile of logs and moss, with the outhouse hidden by alders.

The drawing shows the barn as it looked just a few years ago. Like the roadhouse, it was constructed of round unpeeled spruce logs (saddle-notched at the corners), and had a wood-shake roof.

Daylight shows between most of the logs and there is no sign of chinking. Fortunately, the lack of chinking gave me a good view of the pegs holding logs together around the doors and windows and on the gable end of the building.

The barn has sunk about four feet into the soft ground, making it hard to tell the barn's lower-level windows from doors. Their sills are somewhere below ground level and their tops are now tickled by summer grasses. It is only a matter of time before what is left of the roadhouse buildings collapses completely and merges back into the surrounding forest.

The 239 acre homestead is part of the Chena River State Recreation Area, which was established in 1967. One of the largest undeveloped private inholdings within the recreation area, it was acquired by the State of Alaska through its Alaska Forest Legacy Program in 2004.

Sources:

- Conversation with Don Hymer, member of party surveying Chena Hot Springs Road right-of-way in the winter of 1959-60. 2014
- Fairbanks North Star Borough property records
- "Field Notes of the survey of the Boundary and Meanders of U.S. Survey No. 1683 – Homestead Claim of Alexander J. Johnston." Fred Dahlquist. U.S. Cadastral Survey. 1928
- *Historic Resources in the Fairbanks North Star Borough*, Janet Matheson & Bruce Haldeman, 1981
- "History of the Chena River State Recreation Area." Alaska Department of Natural Resources brochure, 2009

Fairbanks - Downtown, Clay Street

Independent Lumber's Fairbanks warehouse in 1990

# Independent Lumber warehouse a reminder of early lumbering industry

As the town of Fairbanks grew between 1901 and the early 1920s it was not built with brick and stone. The city was far from Outside sources, and shipping space limited. Heavy building materials were generally too expensive to ship, so residents built with local materials when possible.

Wood was the construction material of choice, and Fairbanks had an insatiable appetite for lumber during its early years.

Logs and milled lumber were used to construct buildings, boats and other implements; timbers were needed for bridges and mine tunnels supports; and cordwood was essential to fuel the countless steam engines used at mines, and to heat homes and businesses. Huge wood lots lay scattered about town. One early photo of a cord-wood yard describes it as being 20 acres in size.

The first buildings in Fairbanks were cabins constructed of logs hewn by the builders themselves, but by 1903 local sawmills were supplying lumber. A 1904 photograph shows Fred Noyes' Tanana Mill at the edge of town, about where the Morris Thompson Cultural Center is now.

(The Tanana Mill later moved across the river to "Noyes" slough, where the Golden Valley Electrical Association complex now is on Illinois Street.)

According to a 2003 Fairbanks Daily News-Miner article by Candy Waugaman, four lumber mills supplied the Fairbanks area's needs by 1907. There was Chena Lumber at Chena townsite downriver from Fairbanks, Fairbanks Lumber on Garden Island, the Noyes mill, and Independent Lumber at the east end of Seventh Avenue, on the far side of the city cemetery.

Independent Lumber began as a partnership between Roy Rutherford and Sylvester Widman. A 1909 *Alaska-Yukon* magazine article relates that Rutherford came to Valdez in 1901, spent several years operating a sawmill there, and then moved to Fairbanks.

Widman stampeded to Dawson City in 1898, moved to Eagle after a couple of years and finally landed in Fairbanks about the same time Rutherford did.

In May of 1906 Rutherford bought land on the west bank of the Chena River at the eastern edge of town and began construction of a mill. He went into partnership with Walker in September of that year to form Independent Lumber Company.

For many years they operated a large lumber yard stretching from the city cemetery at Seventh Avenue to 10th Avenue where the Regency Hotel is now. Facilities included a saw and planing mill, garage, offices, two residences, numerous sheds and warehouse.

Logs for the mill were felled in the upper reaches of the Chena River Valley and floated downriver to Fairbanks. An early photo of the sawmill shows an inclined skidway four-logs wide leading up from the river to stacks of unprocessed logs, with the mill building in the background.

The lumber mill was so successful that it opened an office downtown on First Avenue and had an additional office across the river near the railroad yard.

In 1918, it bought out the Tanana Mill. Independent Lumber remained at its eastside location until the 1960s when the business moved to a new site on south Cushman Street (where Independent Rental is now).

The 50-foot by 84-foot timber-frame gable-roofed warehouse shown in the drawing is the mill's only surviving building. It is depicted with its original ship-lap siding and corrugated metal roof. Located at the corner of Clay Street and 8th Avenue, it lay empty and deteriorating for almost 50 years. In 1975, the Borough even assessed it as only being worth salvage value.

However, the building was recently rehabilitated, including replacing the siding and roof. It now houses Automotive Concepts. One can hope that the building, visible from the Steese Expressway, will be around for many years to come.

Sources:

- Buzby and Metcalf photo album. University of Alaska Fairbanks Archives
- *Fairbanks, A city historic building survey*. Janet Matheson. City of Fairbanks. 1985
- *Fairbanks, a Pictorial History*. Claus-M. Naske & Ludwig Rowinski. The Donning Company Publishers. 1981
- "In the woods." Candy Waugaman. in *Fairbanks Daily News-Miner*. 2-23-2003
- "Men and Endeavor in the Tanana Valley." B. B. Metheany. in *Alaska-Yukon* magazine. January 1909
- "Mill stood where hotel is today." Candy Waugaman. in *Fairbanks Daily News-Miner*. 4-23-1995
- Woodrow Johansen Papers. University of Alaska Fairbanks Archives

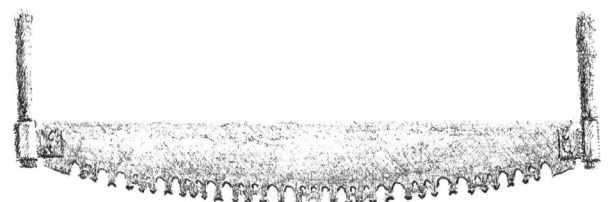

Fairbanks - Downtown, Clay Street

Alexander Barrack's tombstone at the Clay Street Cemetery in 2012

## Clay Street Cemetery helps preserve Fairbanks history

The monument shown in the drawing marks the grave of Alexander Barrack at the Clay Street Cemetery in Fairbanks (Barrack died in 1916). The cemetery is located on a 3½ acre parcel at the end of Fourth and Fifth avenues, and is bounded on the north and south by Third and Seventh avenues and to the east by the Steese Expressway. (Clay Street used to be the east boundary.)

It is a peaceful location, with an arched gateway at the east entrance, and a large open grassy field dotted by grave markers. The expanse is essentially treeless in its southern portion (abutting Seventh Avenue), but tall spruce and birch trees dot the older, northern half of the cemetery.

There are actually relatively few grave markers visible, but that belies the fact there are more than 1,600 graves in the cemetery.

In addition to several general sections, there are nine fraternal and religious burial areas. There are two religious sections: one large Catholic area and a small Jewish one. Fraternal organizations, which were popular in early Fairbanks, are represented by sections for the American Legion, Arctic Brotherhood, Eagles, Elks, Moose, Odd Fellows and Pioneers of Alaska.

According to the National Register of Historic Places Nomination Form for Clay Street Cemetery, it wasn't long after the city's inception that the cemetery was established. The death of Al Foster in October 1903 prompted city fathers to set aside the tract on the eastern edge of town. Between then and 1938 it was the primary burial site for the area. Some of the mining camps around Fairbanks had their own cemeteries, but most burials were at the Clay Street Cemetery. Residents from communities as far away as Flat, Iditarod and Wiseman are buried there.

Burials at the cemetery represent a diverse cross-section of pioneer society, including miners, store keeps, "ladies of the evening," riverboat captains, lawyers and newspaper publishers. Countries represented are just as diverse, since the gold rushes at the beginning of the 20th century lured adventurers from across the globe.

By 1938 the cemetery was nearing capacity and Birch Hill Cemetery was opened. Burials at Clay Street gradually tapered off, and the last regular interment there was in 1978.

Early photos of the cemetery show the area filled with wooden crosses and monuments, as well as numerous wooden grave fences. Over the years however, harsh weather conditions and vandals destroyed most of the wooden grave markers. Coupled with a lack of maintenance by the city, the cemetery was in poor condition by 1982, when it was listed on the National Register of Historic Places.

Although the cemetery was officially closed to new burials by the 1980s, an exception was made in 1995. Irene Sherman (the self-proclaimed "Queen of Fairbanks) was born in Fairbanks in 1911. She was a well-known figure around town, and when she died in February of 1995, the City allowed her to be buried at Clay Street Cemetery.

There have been periodic efforts to revitalize the cemetery. A two-year restoration effort spearheaded by The Rotary Club of Fairbanks resulted in the 2010 dedication of a new stone and wrought-iron gateway at the east entrance to the cemetery. That same year the Clay Street Cemetery Commission was established by the city of Fairbanks to advise the city on matters relating to the "restoration, maintenance and improvement of the ... cemetery."

The city and other groups have undertaken several improvements. Bill Robertson, who is chairman of the cemetery commission, told me that new markers, funded by grants from the City Bed Tax fund, and from Fort Knox and Pogo mines, have been placed on 100 graves, and the city hopes to erect another 300 to 400 grave markers in the near future. The Pioneers of Alaska have also placed 121 new markers on the graves of pioneers. In 2012 the city installed an underground water system at the cemetery, and a new information kiosk, built from lumber donated by Spenard Builders, was installed in 2014.

Sources:

- "Clay Street Cemetery National Register of Historic Places Nomination Form." Karen Armstrong. National Park Service. 1982
- "Clay Street cemetery to get new granite markers for 35 graves." Dermot Cole. in *Fairbanks Daily News-Miner*. 8-4-2012
- Conversation with Erica Miller, Pioneers of Alaska. 2013
- Conversation with Bill Robertson, chairman of Clay Street Cemetery Commission. 2013
- "Rotary Club funds renovation of historic Clay Street Cemetery." Reba Lean. in *Fairbanks Daily News-Miner*. 12-26-2012

Fairbanks - Downtown, Cushman Street

Fairbanks City Hall in 2013

## Main School, now City Hall, is a Fairbanks landmark

Soon after Fairbanks was established, residents began clamoring for schools. In the fall of 1903 (even before the city was incorporated), a small private school opened. Thirteen students and their teacher met in a small cabin at the corner of Wendell and Noble streets. Unfortunately, lack of funds closed the school just before Christmas.

After the city's incorporation on November 3, 1903, a school board was elected and a public school opened the next spring in a rented facility near Lacey Street and Third Avenue.

The next fall 50 students moved into a newly constructed school building at the corner of 2nd Avenue and Noble Street. By 1906 the number of students had swelled to 150, and a second floor plus a classroom at the rear of the building had been added.

The Fairbanks school population continued to grow, and in 1907, a new two-story frame schoolhouse with full basement was built on Cushman Street between Eighth and Ninth avenues, the site of the present Old Main School. (A few school board members objected to the location, saying it was too far out of town.)

The new school building had wide front steps surmounted by a portico, and a hipped roof topped by an open belfry. In a town composed primarily of one story log cabins, the two-story school seemed a magnificent building, likened by one local pastor to an English cathedral.

The school, along with a 1929 addition, served Fairbanks children until 1932 when fire consumed the building. The structure was a total loss, and classes were moved to nearby churches and civic organization facilities until a new facility was constructed.

The old wood-frame school was overcrowded, so when plans for a new fire-proof school building were started, increased space was also a concern. In 1933 construction began on a 35,500-square-foot, reinforced-concrete building on the site of the old building. Plans for the new school were drawn up by the engineer responsible for the Federal Building then under construction in Fairbanks, and the school building shares many of the same Art Deco exterior design elements.

As originally constructed, the building had three stories with a ground-floor daylight basement. The building faced Cushman Street, with classrooms and office on all three floors and a 4,000-square-foot gymnasium extending to the rear. It was officially opened on Jan. 22, 1934.

A burgeoning student population meant the addition of a south wing in 1939 and a north wing in 1948. With both additions, close attention was paid to blending in with the old exterior.

However, consistency between old and new interior floor plans was not maintained. Differing floor levels and confusing connecting hallways made the interior a maze. In his booklet, *The Spirit of Old Main, a History of the Old Main School*, Chris Allen related a joke popular at the school which "suggested that any senior who was able to find his way from the center of the building to the outside should be handed a graduation certificate."

Main School remained the Fairbanks School District's only school until 1951 when the district began building schools in outlying areas. By 1959 only junior high students remained downtown.

All students had been moved to other facilities by 1976 and the school district's administration offices moved in. The district's offices remained there until 1993 when a new administrative center was completed. Main School was then relinquished to the city. The building's ground floor windows were boarded up and the heat was turned off.

The next December (1994) the city began moving its offices into the building. A year of no maintenance and no utilities meant a great deal of work needed to be done on the building.

Old Main School was placed on the National Register of Historic Places in 1990. In keeping with the building's historical importance, the city has a goal of restoring the building to its original floor plan.

Some major renovations have already been accomplished, such as fixing the roof, refinishing the gym floor and bleachers, replacing all the windows that had been boarded up, and opening up all the hallways. Much of the credit for the work already accomplished goes to former City Mayor, Jerry Cleworth, who attended Main School as a student.

Sources:

- Conversation with Jerry Cleworth, former Fairbanks City Mayor. 2014
- *Fairbanks, a City Historic Building Survey*. Janet Matheson. City of Fairbanks. 1985
- *Our Schools, a History of Elementary and Secondary Public Education in the Fairbanks Area*. Fairbanks North Star Borough. 1989
- *The Spirit of Old Main, a History of the Old Main School – 1932-1995*. Chis Allen. 1995
- "National Register of Historic Places Nomination Form." Russell Sackett. National Park Service. 1990

Fairbanks - Downtown, Cushman Street

Old Federal Building in Fairbanks in about 2000

## Old Federal Building anchors downtown district

The book, *Ghosts of the Gold Rush*, recounts that many long-time Fairbanks residents believed the reason Fairbanks prospered and Chena City (at the confluence of the Chena and Tanana Rivers and consequently in a better location for steamboat traffic) failed was because of the machinations of E.T. Barnette and Judge James Wickersham.

Barnette and Wickersham met serendipitously at St. Michael in 1902 where Barnette, who still had dreams of starting a trading post at Tanana Crossing, was supervising the construction of a shallow-draft steamship to transport him up the Tanana River. Wickersham was impressed with Barnette and told him if he named his trading post after Senator Charles W. Fairbanks of Indiana (whom Wickersham admired) he would do everything in his power to help Barnette succeed.

Felix Pedro's discovery of gold in a tributary of the Chena River the same year changed Barnette's plans for moving his trading post, and the new town on the Chena became Fairbanks. When Wickersham moved the Third Judicial District's headquarters from Eagle to Fairbanks in 1903, the new courthouse and federal jail were built on land donated by Barnette. Old timers believed it was the government presence, represented by the federal courthouse, that ensured Fairbanks' survival.

The original wood-frame courthouse burned down, along with most of the downtown business district in 1906 and was quickly replaced with another wood-frame structure built with green lumber. Coupled with a poor foundation, inadequate load-bearing walls, and a poor design, the building deteriorated rapidly and by the 1910s residents were clamoring for a new building.

After repeated requests, in 1931 the federal government appointed George N. Ray, a prominent Washington D.C. architect, to design the building, and allocated $424,000 for its construction. The construction contract was let in March of 1932 and in August 1934 the building was dedicated by Fairbanks Mayor E. B. Collins, Alaskan Congressional Delegate Anthony J. Dimond, and Second Assistant Postmaster General Harlee Branch.

The courthouse building, which also housed the post office and other federal agencies, is shown in the drawing. The large reinforced concrete building is 128 feet long and 92 feet wide, occupying an entire city block on Cushman Street between Second and Third avenues. It has three full floors with a small central section rising an additional level.

The building is decidedly Art Deco in design and use of materials. It is symmetrical, composed of three sections, with each section having three bays. The design elements are rectilinear, and the building utilizes repeated low relief geometric decorations.

Aluminum, which was a popular decorative material during the Art Deco period, is used extensively in the building. The metal was relatively rare and hard to manufacture during most of the 1800s – in fact it was once called the Prince of Metals because of its scarcity. New production methods at the end of the 19th century brought it out of the luxury market and into common usage as a design and architectural element.

Incised aluminum panels are used on the old federal building to decorate the parapet and between the window bays. The front entrance also has cast aluminum doors and aluminum transom grills cast in the shape of eagles. The four large wall-mounted entry lanterns beside the front doors also used to be aluminum but they have been replaced.

The federal court, post office, and other federal agencies occupied the building until 1977, when they moved to a new federal building on 12th Avenue near the Steese Expressway.

The old federal building is now privately owned and is occupied by private offices, but it is still a splendid anchor for the downtown area.

Sources:

- *Buildings of Alaska*. Alison Hoagland. Oxford University Press. 1993
- *Fairbanks, a City Historic Building Survey.* Janet Matheson. City of Fairbanks. 1985
- "Fairbanks Federal Building, National Register of Historic Places Registration Form." Victoria Taylor. National Park Service. 1978
- *Ghosts of the Gold Rush, A Walking Tour of Fairbanks*. Terrence Cole. Tanana-Yukon Historical Society. 1977

Fairbanks - Downtown, 3rd Avenue

Gilcher Building in the fall of 2013

## Gilcher Building displays city's last old-time storefront

The Gilcher Building at 524 Third Avenue in downtown Fairbanks (where River City Café is located) is the last example in the city of the storefront style found across the United States in the early 1900s. During that period, stores typically had recessed doorways and large plate-glass windows fronting the buildings' first floors.

Janet Matheson's book, *Fairbanks, a City Historic Building Survey,* states that similarly configured storefronts in the early 1900s usually had ornate metal facades on the upper levels. However, by the time the Gilcher Building was constructed, architectural fashion tended towards cleaner, simpler designs. The building's Third Avenue entrance (on its south side) reflects this, and its cornice consists of wide unadorned boards with thin, plain molding. The building did originally have a brick-patterned metal façade on its east side, though.

William H. Gilcher, who was a sheet metal worker, owned the building. Gilcher came north from California in the 1898 stampede to the Klondike. Documents in the Yukon Archives indicate he worked as a tin smith in Dawson City until 1904, when the newly established gold camp at Fairbanks beckoned. By 1907 he was operating the Tanana Sheet Metal Works on Turner Street between First and Second Avenues.

Some time later he moved his business to Third Avenue. The Fairbanks North Star Borough Historic Preservation Commission states that his building on Third Avenue was constructed in 1931. However, Janet Matheson's book indicates that he was operating from the Third Avenue location at least as early as 1927. Matheson speculates that the building there began as a single-story structure some time before 1920, the second story was added during the 1920s, and the Third Avenue facade was constructed in the 1930s.

The Gilcher building originally stretched from Second to Third Avenue. Gilcher operated his metal working business out of the Second Avenue side and an appliance business off Third Avenue. Apartments were located upstairs.

Gilcher retired from the business and moved to California in 1948. In the years after his departure the building gradually deteriorated, and the northern half of the building (facing Second Avenue) was eventually torn down.

The Nordale Hotel used to be adjacent to the Gilcher Building. (It was where the Big Ray's parking lot is now.) When the Nordale burned down in 1972 the Gilcher Building was in disrepair, failing to meet city fire and safety codes. The city, wanting to improve the block, prodded the building's owners into undertaking remedial work, saving the building from destruction. The corrective measures included removing the metal siding on the east side of the building and converting the upstairs residences into offices and storage.

Vivian Stiver bought the building in 2004 and extensively renovated it for use as a cafe. She told me that during the initial renovation, workers carted off 400 to 500 pounds of sawdust that had filled the space between floors.

She also said that there used to be a large side door into the building where the 1st floor windows facing the parking lot are now. When rehabbing that wall she discovered scorch marks on the structural supports, presumably where embers from the Nordale hotel fire fell through the doorway into the Gilcher Building.

Stiver replaced the building's electrical and plumbing systems, and changed the interior layout considerably. In a nod to the building's historic nature, she left the original timber jousts and uprights, and plank flooring in the café part of the building exposed. (Stiver lamented that because of the continued deterioration of the original planking she would probably have to eventually put new flooring in.

She replaced the plate-glass windows facing Third Avenue with slightly smaller energy-efficient windows, but kept the original detailing around the Third Avenue doors. Stiver also restored the second floor to residential space. is still original though.

Stiver sold the building in 2018. The new owners have left the interior pretty much untouched, except for replacing the worn planking with similar flooring. They removed the awning over the Third Avenue, but have kept the detailing around the windows and doors, so you can still see traces of the old 1930s-era building

.

Sources:

- Conversation with Vivian Stiver, current owner. 2014
- *Fairbanks, a City Historic Building Survey*. Janet Matheson. City of Fairbanks. 1985
- Fairbanks North Star Borough Historic Preservation Commission signage at Gilcher Building
- Fairbanks North Star Borough property records
- Obituary for W. H. "Billy" Gilcher, in *Alaska Sportsman* magazine. December 1963
- William Gilcher Collection. Yukon Archives

Fairbanks - Downtown, 2nd Avenue

Empress Theater as it looked in 2005, when the second floor still had one of its original multi-pane windows

## Empress Theater brought several firsts to Fairbanks

Austin "Cap" Lathrop never cut corners. He believed that doing a job right the first time saved money in the long run.

When it came to constructing buildings he also believed in substance—the more substance the better. So when Alaska builders started using reinforced concrete for construction projects, he began using it, too.

Lathrop owned a chain of Empress Theaters: in Cordova, Valdez, Seward and Anchorage. In 1916 he successfully constructed his Anchorage theater using reinforced concrete, so when Cap decided to build a theater in Fairbanks a decade later it was only natural to try it here.

Concrete had already been used in Fairbanks to a limited extent. The Fairbanks Exploration Company office building is constructed of locally made concrete blocks.) However, no one locally had ever built with solid concrete. Many thought that concrete foundations would buckle when subjected to frost heaves, or that concrete would simply crumble in the region's frigid winter temperatures.

Lathrop was undeterred. He did change the building's design before construction began though. According to Elizabeth Tower's book, *Alaska's First Homegrown Millionaire*, Lathrop originally planned to erect a four-story structure, with the top two stories envisioned as a hotel. By the time construction began in April of 1927 the plans had been scaled back to just the two-story theater. Construction was finished that summer.

Tower's book also relates that even after construction was finished, some people were dubious about the building's durability. Federal inspectors checked the building annually for several years. Finally satisfied, in 1932 the federal government built its new Fairbanks federal building with reinforced concrete.

The Empress Theater's grand opening was August 25, 1927. A *Fairbanks Daily News-Miner* article written the next day stated that over 1300 people attended the gala. The theater had two performances in its 670-seat auditorium that evening, and each performance was sold out.

One of the Empress's attractions was its 2/7 Kimball organ, the first pipe organ in Interior Alaska. The Kimball had two "manuals" (keyboards), and seven ranks (groupings) of pipes.

All told the organ had about 500 pipes. Just for comparison, the concert organ at the Davis Concert Hall has about 2,000 pipes. Of course, being a theater organ, the Empress's Kimball also had percussion attachments such as drums, cymbals and glockenspiel.

As originally built, the Empress had a balanced front facade. The first floor had recessed double doors on either side of a large expanse of plate-glass window. The second floor looked much the same as it does now, with four equally spaced windows—the two inmost windows with decorative arches. Above were two small circular vents, and a cornice with denticulated (tooth-like) ornamentation.

The theater was remodeled in the 1950s, with major exterior changes to the front facade. The entrance on the right side of the building was converted into a small rental retail space. The central window area was reduced, and the entrance on the left was expanded. A marquee over the entrance was added and 50s-style neon signs were installed on top of the marquee.

In 1961 the Empress closed down and was assimilated into the Co-op Drug Store, another Fairbanks institution. The neon signs were removed, the first floor front façade changed to its present configuration, and the auditorium, which spanned two stories, was torn out and converted into two levels of retail space and offices.

The organ was removed and eventually found a home in the Steak and Pipes restaurant adjacent to the Big I Pub. When that restaurant closed down the organ was put into storage and currently sits at of another of Cap Lathrop's theaters – the Lacey, now the Fairbanks Ice Museum.

After Co-op Drugs closed, the building became part of the Co-op Plaza. The Fairbanks Community Museum now makes the second floor of the Empress Theater Building its home

Sources:

- *Alaska's First Homegrown Millionaire, Life and Times of Cap Lathrop*. Elizabeth Tower. Publication Consultants. 2006
- Buildings of Alaska. Alison K. Hoagland. Oxford University Press. 1993
- *Fairbanks, a City Historic Building Survey*. Janet Matheson. City of Fairbanks. 1985
- "Northwest Theatre Organ History." from Puget Sound Theatre Organ Society website. 1998-2014
- "Thirteen hundred witness opening of new Empress." *Fairbanks Daily News-Miner.* August 26, 1927

Fairbanks - Downtown, 2nd Avenue

Cora Madole's cabin on Second Avenue as it looked in 1990

## Second Avenue cabin was a safe haven for Clara Rust in 1909

When 18-year-old Clara Hickman first set foot in Fairbanks in the fall of 1908, it wasn't by stepping from a horse-drawn stage just arrived over the Valdez-Fairbanks Trail. Neither was it by walking down the gang-plank of a steamboat at one of the city's docks. Her first steps were from a windswept rowboat onto the Chena River's cold, muddy bank.

Clara had indeed come by steamer. Her 32-day journey entailed traveling by steamship from Seattle to St. Michael (near the mouth of the Yukon River), and then by stern-wheeled riverboat up the Yukon, Tanana, and Chena Rivers.

Unfortunately, Clara was traveling in September and there was already frost on the ground. The water level of the Chena River was dropping as winter approached, and the small steamboat she was a passenger on (with an inexperienced captain) kept running aground. When the steamer grounded one last time within sight of Fairbanks, the captain acquiesced to frustrated passengers and lowered a lifeboat to take people ashore.

Clara's family already lived in Fairbanks, so she had a comforting cabin waiting for her. Zach Hickman (her father), was an itinerant newspaperman and ran the Daily News, one of three papers in Fairbanks. He and Clara's mother and younger sister lived in a small cabin on 8th Avenue, then the edge of town.

Clara quickly adjusted to Fairbanks, obtaining a job at Mary Anderson's Dry Goods and Dress Shop. Since the Hickman cabin, like most in town, did not have running water, the Hickmans took baths at the First Avenue Bathhouse. Her mother became friends with Cora Madole, who owned the bathhouse, and the two Hickman sisters went there often. During this period Clara slipped into the community's social life and fell in love with Mrs. Madole's son, Jess Rust, who mined on Pedro Creek.

Clara's parents were not happily married, and it wasn't long before her mother and sister returned to Seattle. After Clara's mother wrote requesting a divorce, her father also departed. Clara stayed, however, knowing there was little in Seattle for her and wishing to be near Jess. Before leaving town her father deeded the family's cabin to her.

Clara was still working at Mary Anderson's store but living alone in the family cabin. The empty cabin eventually proved too much for Clara, and she ended up rooming with Mrs. Madole at the bathhouse.

According to Jo Anne Wold's book, *This Old House; the story of Clara Rust*, Clara woke one morning in late 1909 to a frigid bathhouse. The boiler had broken, and despite work done on it during the following day, the bathhouse's pipes froze and burst. Mrs. Madole was out of business.

Fortunately, Mrs. Madole also owned the small cabin (shown in the drawing) at 828 Second Avenue, directly behind the bathhouse. The cabin happened to be vacant so Clara and Mrs. Madole quickly switched residences.

When Cora and Clara moved in, the cabin was still in its original configuration—a 16-foot by 34-foot structure made of peeled logs with dovetailed corners. It had a living room, dining room and kitchen on the first floor, and two tiny bedrooms upstairs, tucked under the eaves. Normally, such an arrangement is referred to as 1 ½ story, but there is so little headroom upstairs in the cabin that the Fairbanks North Star Borough Appraiser's Office calls it a 1 ¼ story cabin. A shed-roofed addition was tacked onto the rear of the cabin at a later date.

Clara and Mrs. Madole only lived there a short while. Clara married Jess in 1910 and moved to the creeks, and Mrs. Madole mortgaged the Second Avenue cabin to help bankroll their mining. When Jess's mine on Little Eldorado Creek flooded, they lost everything, including the Second Avenue cabin.

The drawing shows the cabin as it looked in 1990, and you can see the bathhouse in the background. The cabin is still standing. Clara and Jess continued to live in the Fairbanks area and their life is chronicled in Jo Anne Wold's book. A recommended read.

Sources:

- *Fairbanks, a City Historic Building Survey*. Janet Matheson. City of Fairbanks. 1985
- Fairbanks North Star Borough property records
- *More than Petticoats: Remarkable Alaska Women*. Cherry Lyon Jones. TwoDot Books. 2006
- *This Old House: the story of Clara Rust, Alaska Pioneer*. Jo Anne Wold. Alaska Northwest Publishing. 1981

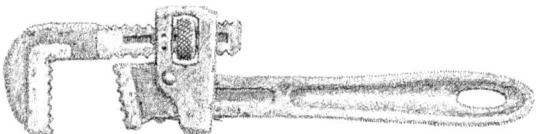

Fairbanks - Downtown, Cowles Street

Blue Crystal Water Company well house on Cowles Street in 2013

# Blue Crystal Water Company delivered tasty water around early Fairbanks

We take plentiful clean water for granted, but in early Fairbanks, clean water was a limited commodity. Most wells in Fairbanks were shallow — yielding foul-tasting, organic-rich water. Consequently, many residents had water delivered.

There were other water delivery services around Fairbanks in the early 1900s, but Fred Musjerd's was the best known. He had several wells on his property between Eighth and Ninth avenues on Cowles Street. They produced good quality water, and during the 1920s and 30s he operated the Blue Crystal Water Company.

According to Cheryl Egan, who, with her husband, Michael, now owns the property, a well was located inside the garage on the corner of Cowles Street and Ninth Avenue.

This building, which can be seen behind the well house, was formerly the White Seal Dock. It was originally on the Chena River waterfront, but sometime during the 1920s Musjerd moved the structure to its present location.

In his early water hauling years Musjerd ran a horse-drawn water wagon out of this building. During the summer the wagon sported wheels and in winter Musjerd ran it on sled runners.

Winter photos show a wood-sided wagon with the words "Blue Crystal Water Co. – No Limit" printed on the side. Sticking out of the top of the wagon's mid-section was a small smoke-belching stove used to keep the water from freezing. There were two spigots at the back of the wagon for filling pails, with several pails usually made from recycled Hills Bros. 5-gallon coffee tins.

Some winter photos show the wagon encased in ice. According to Dermot Cole's book, *Historic Fairbanks, an Illustrated History*, Musjerd, who was a large man, was even more imposing during winter, muffled in a large fur coat and hat, "with frost or small icicles hanging from his walrus mustache." In later years Musjerd replaced the horse-drawn wagon with a truck.

Customers placed empty 5-gallon pails outside their doors and Musjerd replaced them with full ones. In a 1993 interview, long-time Fairbanks resident Marie Haggard said that residents displayed cards in their windows indicating how many pails of water they needed. The water cost 10 cents per pail, but Haggard also related that customers set out bingles (tokens purchased in advance) to pay for their water.

Another well was located in the well house shown in the drawing. According to borough records this building was built in the mid 1930s. It is an 18' x 24' wood-frame structure with beveled wood siding and metal roofing, most of it original.

During the 1930s Musjerd also built a house on his property, similar in construction to the well house. Both are what Janet Matheson, author of *A Fairbanks City Historic Survey*, calls "Pioneer Neoclassical," a take-off on American Neoclassicism in which elements from classical Greek and Roman architecture were melded with contemporary building materials and designs. Neoclassicism was popular between 1900 and 1940, and there are several other buildings of similar construction in town.

The house is still there, and Musjerd installed a third well in the house basement. As built, his home was a two-story 15' x 36' gable-roofed house with the same siding and roofing as the well house.

The Egans doubled the house's size in the 1980s by essentially constructing a similarly proportioned house beside the existing structure. The addition matched the original's styling. Cheryl saved all the doors and molding taken down during construction and painstakingly re-finished them for use in the newly remodeled house.

Michael Egan told me that some people have urged him to tear down the well house and old garage. Fortunately he has ignored them, saving these little-known but important elements from Fairbanks past.

Sources:

- Conversations with Cheryl and Michael Egan, current owners. 2013
- *Fairbanks, a City Historic Survey*. Janet Matheson. City of Fairbanks. 1985
- *Fairbanks, a Pictorial History*. Claus-M. Naske & Ludwig Rowinski. The Donning Company Publishers. 1981
- Fairbanks North Star Borough property records
- *Historic Fairbanks, an Illustrated History*. Dermot Cole, Historic Publishing Network. 2002
- Marie Haggard interview, recorded by Margaret Van Cleve on September 15, 1993. Oral History Collection, University of Alaska Fairbanks Archives
- Photos of Blue Crystal Water Company water wagon. Charles Cann photographer. Alaska State Library – Historical Collections

Fairbanks - Downtown, Cowles Street

White Seal Dock in the fall of 2012

# White Seal Dock a leftover from Fairbanks early waterfront

According to the book, *Fairbanks, a City Historic Building Survey,* few of Fairbanks' early commercial buildings remain. Most were destroyed by the numerous fires and floods that plagued early Fairbanks. Others were torn down to make way for newer structures.

One of the survivors is the building known as the White Seal Dock. It originally stood on the Chena River waterfront but is now at the corner of 9th Avenue and Cowles Street. (The address is actually 821 8th Avenue.)

During the steamboat era in Fairbanks (up until about 1920) there were numerous docks along the waterfront. The two largest were the Northern Commercial Company Dock (in front of what is now the Key Bank parking lot) and the Pioneer Dock (in front of the present day Bridgewater Hotel). One of the smaller docks, the White Seal, was next in line, between Wickersham and Cowles streets.

The drawing shows the White Seal Dock as it looks now, which in layout is similar to how it was during its waterfront years. However, in old photographs it appears that only 1/3 of the building (to the right in the drawing) was enclosed, and the rest of the structure just provided covered storage. Apparently, after it was moved, that part of the building was also enclosed.

"White Seal" references the steamboat White Seal (named after a character in Rudyard Kipling's *Jungle Book*). The ship was launched from Fairbanks in 1905 and was the first registered vessel built along the Tanana River.

At 97 feet long, the White Seal was less than half the size of some steamboats plying the Yukon and Tanana rivers. However, these smaller steamboats were essential in reaching the shallow headwaters of the major rivers, and serving side rivers such as the Kantishna.

E.T. Barnette was prevented from reaching his intended destination, Tanana Crossing, when the 140-foot Lavelle Young couldn't get past the Tanana River's Bates Rapids (just upstream from the mouth of the Chena River). However, smaller sternwheelers routinely steamed up the Tanana much farther in later years. If Barnette had been aboard a smaller vessel, who knows what the history of the Tanana Valley would be now.

The White Seal's name appeared in newspaper articles and government reports until about 1912, when it was apparently sidelined. Ownership was transferred to the White Pass and Yukon Route Railroad in 1915 and to the Alaska Railroad in 1925, but it seems the vessel never operated again.

The Fairbanks waterfront changed dramatically after steamboating ended. The docks disappeared, and most of the associated building were torn down or recycled. Sometime in the 1920s the White Seal Dock building was moved down Cowles Street by Fred Musjerd, who owned the Blue Crystal Well water hauling business. Fred's well house was between Eighth and Ninth avenues on Cowles Street, and he moved the White Seal Dock there to use as a garage.

The book, *Historic Fairbanks, an Illustrated History*, relates a story about Musjerd told by Tom Hering. In the early years of Musjerd's business he hauled water by horse-drawn wagon. Musjerd bought a truck in the 1920s, and quickly became known as the worst driver in Fairbanks. Fred talked to his truck the same way he talked to his horses, and supposedly ran the truck through the end of the garage once because it wouldn't stop when he called out, "Whoa!"

The property's current owners, Cheryl and Michael Egan, told me that after Musjerd sold the business, Sig Wold used the garage for his freighting business. It is still in relatively good condition and a rare example of early warehouse construction in Fairbanks.

Sources:

- Conversation with Cheryl and Michael Egan, current owners. 2013
- *Fairbanks, a City Historic Survey*. Janet Matheson. City of Fairbanks. 1985
- *H. W. McCurdy Marine History of the Pacific Northwest*. Edited by Gordon Newell. Superior Publishing. 1966
- *Historic Fairbanks, an Illustrated History*. Dermot Cole. Historic Publishing Network. 2002
- *Steamboats on the Chena*. Basil Heddricks & Susan Savage. Epicenter Press. 1988
- *Yukon River Steamboats*. Stan Cohen. Pictorial Histories Publishing. 1982

Fairbanks - Downtown, Cowles Street

Mary Lee Davis House in the fall of 2000, before restorations began

## Mary Lee Davis House – from plush early Fairbanks home to modern B&B

In today's world of mega-houses, the wood-frame bungalow at 410 Cowles Street known as the Mary Lee Davis House doesn't stand out, but in early Fairbanks, this "cottage" was one of the most elegant houses in town.

According to the Borough's Commission on Historic Preservation, it was built in 1916 by Arthur Williams (who owned the Arcade Café) for his new bride, Lucille. Depending on who tells the story, Lucille was either a young socialite visiting Fairbanks with her family when she met Williams, or a "good-time girl" whom Williams reformed. In either case, she evidently needed enticement to endure Interior Alaska, and Williams provided it in the form of a grand home.

The 32-foot by 48-foot 1 ½ story house was probably based on plans from one of the builders' guides popular at the time. It has five rooms on the main floor, three upstairs (each with a dormer window), and basement. Some of the luxuries built into the house were oak floors, doors and trim; leaded glass windows; indoor plumbing (with elaborate porcelain fixtures); and a large veranda running along the entire front of the house, which faced Cowles Street. It was set back from the street in the middle of a large yard, unusual in early Fairbanks.

Williams "imported" workmen and much of the finish material for the job from Seattle. In addition to the house, the workmen also built a 20-foot by 20-foot attached garage and a small heated greenhouse.

Arthur and Lucille only enjoyed the house for three years. In May 1919, just a few months after a disastrous fire destroyed much of the downtown business district (including the Arcade Café) Arthur died of heart disease. Lucille quickly sold the house and moved to Seattle.

The next owners were Allen and Mary Lee Davis. Allen was a mining engineer, sent by the U.S. Bureau of Mines to open a mining experiment station in Fairbanks, and Mary was a writer. Together they fixed up the still unfinished house.

Mary wrote three non-fiction books about Alaska, and enjoyed talking about her home in them. In her first Alaska book, *We are Alaskans*, she wrote that they, "bought and completed a frame bungalow that had staunch double walls filled in between with several inches of sawdust, to make it warm in winter and cool in summer. This was really a charming cottage, gray painted, green roofed, with wide and spacious porch, window-boxes full of bright blossoms, hanging baskets with flowering vines in them, and the house was set back restfully from the street in a lawn of smooth-clipped grass that was our particular pride, for lawns were a true luxury and a daring experiment in this land of moss and under-frozen soil."

Mary also wrote that they equipped the house "with every electrical devise we could have to make our living easy and less complicated." Other niceties they installed (which Mary credited to her engineer husband), included the first open fireplace in Fairbanks, open oak bookcases on either side of the fireplace, a built-in vacuum system with fireproof bin in the basement, and the first coal-fired furnace in Fairbanks.

The Davises sold their home to the Fairbanks Exploration Company in 1927, which used it to house company executives. It also became a popular venue for hosting company parties and gatherings.

The house was added to the National Register of Historic Places in 1982. It underwent major renovations between 2003 and 2007, and is now owned by Van Newstrom and William Albee, who operate it as Alaska Heritage House Bed and Breakfast.

Van gave my wife and me a tour of the house and it is very elegant, filled with authentic period detailing and furnishings  It also still contains many of the house's original accoutrements, such as the porcelain fixtures in the upstairs bathroom, and a huge coal-fired furnace (non-functional) in the basement.

Sources:

- *A place of belonging: five founding women of Fairbanks, Alaska*. Phyllis Demuth Movius. University of Alaska Press. 2009
- Conversation with Van Newstrom, current owner. 2013
- *Fairbanks, a City Historic Building Survey*. Janet Matheson. City of Fairbanks. 1985
- Fairbanks North Star Borough property records
- "Mary Lee Davis House, National Register of Historic Places Inventory-Nomination Form." Carol A. Rawlinson. National Park Service. 1979
- "The House that love built…and rebuilt." Mara Severin. *Alaska Home Magazine*. Spring 2009
- *We are Alaskans*. Mary Lee Cadwell Davis. W.A. Wilde Company. 1931

Fairbanks - Downtown, 6th Avenue

Patty House in 2009

## Patty House is a testament to city's coming of age

The 1¾ story house at 909 Sixth Ave. is very much a product of its time. Referred to as the Patty House, it was built in 1937, several years after Fairbanks successfully emerged from a decade-long economic slump that dated back to the early 1910s.

An area-wide revival began with the Alaska Railroad's completion in 1923. The Alaska Agricultural College and School of Mines opened its doors in 1922, and the Fairbanks Exploration Company commenced gold dredging operations in the late 1920s. Combined with the gradual rise of the price of gold (controlled by the federal government) to almost $35 per ounce by 1935, Fairbanks experienced a new economic prosperity.

Buoyed by the city's improved fortunes and confident in its future, residents were replacing their log cabins with more expensive wood-frame houses. Many of the more affluent were building period revival homes. The styling of these houses harkened back to earlier classical architectural periods for inspiration.

The Sixth Avenue structure is one such house. With its steeply pitched gable roof, prominently displayed massive chimney, arched entrance doorway, narrow multi-paned windows, and asymmetrical floor plan, the Patty House has many of the elements of Tudor Revival, which was inspired by English architecture from 1500 to 1559. This style was very popular in the United States up through the 1930s.

The house was built by Ernest Patty and his wife, Kathryn. The two had arrived in Fairbanks shortly before the college opened its doors in September 1922. Ernest was the new school's professor of geology and mining.

Ernest became dean of the college in 1925. In 1935, he resigned from the school (by then the University of Alaska) to become general manager of a private company that as part of its activities developed gold dredging at Coal and Woodchopper Creeks, which are tributaries of the Yukon River.

His business venture was successful and two years later the Pattys built their dream home.

The house was actually constructed around an earlier log cabin that had been owned by Fairbanks resident, George Moody. Current owner, Eric Bergh, told me the cabin was erected or perhaps moved onto the site, which was built up with ash and clinkers from the Northern Commercial Company's power plant just a few blocks away.

Moody's cabin was a large multi-room structure — about the size of the present house's first floor, which is 26 feet by 41 feet. That cabin is still firmly embedded in the walls, invisible to the eye. A 13-foot by 18-foot extension at the rear of the house used to be a garage. Bergh told me the slight width of the garage indicated it may pre-date the 1937 construction.

The 10-foot by 19-foot room to the west under the curved sloping roof was part of the 1937 construction, and originally had a floor that canted away from the house.

Bergh thinks that perhaps it was originally a covered side porch, another element typical of Tudor Revival houses.

According to the book, Fairbanks, A Historic Building Survey, Mrs. Patty is supposed to have designed and planted the native species garden that still surrounds the house. The Patty's new home was featured in a 1937 issue of House Beautiful magazine.

The Pattys only lived in the house until 1943 when they moved to Seattle. It was then occupied by Essie Dale. A year after she died in 1965, Ralph and Kathryn LaSalle bought the house.

The LaSalle's daughter, Laura, and her husband, Eric Bergh, bought the house in 1999. They have been gradually restoring it, so it should remain a testament to Fairbanks coming-of-age for many years.

Sources:

- Conversations with Eric and Laura Bergh, current owners
- Fairbanks, A City Historic Building Survey. Janet Matheson. City of Fairbanks. 1985
- "Fairbanks Classic; the Patty House." in Tanana-Yukon Historical Society Newsletter. Vol. 4, No. 4, April 1999
- Fairbanks North Star Borough property records
- North Country Challenge. Ernest Patty. D. McKay Company. 1969

Fairbanks - Downtown, 1st Avenue

Claypool/Berry House in early winter of 2011

## Claypool/Berry House a reminder of Fairbanks judicial history

When James Wickersham was appointed the sole judge for Alaska's new Third Judicial District in 1900, he was not a lone ranger tasked with bringing justice to Interior Alaska. As a representative of the U.S. government, he needed a considerable staff to manage the far-flung district, which covered 300,000 square miles.

According to the 1901 report from Alaska's governor to the U.S. Department of the Interior, the court's staff in Eagle alone (the district's headquarters) consisted of the judge, marshal, deputy marshal, U.S. attorney, assistant attorney, clerk, stenographer, and commissioner. Additional court representatives, including 15 commissioners, were scattered across the district, from Kodiak in the south, to the Colville River in the north, Unalakleet in the west, and Eagle in the east.

Commissioners were court-appointed representatives — the equivalent of magistrates or justices of the peace. They provided the court with local representatives, albeit with limited powers and jurisdiction.

One of those commissioners was Charles Claypool (who, by the way, was from Tacoma, Washington, as was Judge Wickersham). Claypool came to Alaska in 1900 and was first stationed in Circle City. He transferred to Eagle in 1901 and then to Fairbanks when the court's headquarters moved in 1904.

Claypool was accompanied to Fairbanks by his wife, Annie Cowles Claypool, and their two children. They built a house on the outskirts of town at 1309 First Avenue, across from what is now the Aurora Power Plant.

In the early 1900s the bank of the Chena River across First Avenue from the Claypool house was where steamboats were pulled up on "ways" (long wooden rails) during the winter. Early winter-time photos of Fairbanks looking west show the Claypool house surrounded by log cabins, with beached steamboats in the background.

The house's exact year of construction is a bit of a mystery. Borough records estimate it was built in 1922, but other records indicate 1911. However, biographies of Claypool, including one in Volume II of *Biographies of Alaska-Yukon Pioneers*, state that Claypool left Alaska in 1909 and was the city attorney for Olympia, Wash., until 1913, when he was appointed as judge to the Washington State Superior Court.

A photograph in the Alaska Historical Society collection shows Charles Claypool and family in front of their house and is dated to about 1906, which fits in with the claim that the Claypool house is one of the earliest frame houses in Fairbanks.

The house is a square-built structure, with a basic design similar to the Joslin House on Cowles Street. The Claypool house is a 24' by 22' two-story frame home with a hipped roof, and is symmetrically designed with a centrally located front door. What is now an arctic entry was originally a covered front porch supported by Doric columns.

Otis Berry, Sr., purchased the house in 1925. He jacked it up during the 1930s and put in a center cross-beam salvaged from an abandoned steamboat beached across First Avenue.

During the next 50 years, Berry's son-in-law, Robert Young; and his son, Otis Berry, Jr.; built a shed-roofed kitchen addition at the rear of the house, replaced windows, changed the siding from ship-lap to bevel, and enclosed the front porch. The second-story windows remain much the same as they were originally, while the first-story windows on the front of the house have been replaced. In recent years a deck was installed over the rear addition, but the house remains faithful to its original design.

By the way, the inverted-u-shaped window at the rear of the house on the second floor is not original. That part of the second floor used to be a bedroom, but was converted into a bathroom. The window is built of glass blocks and wraps around a wall cabinet over the toilet.

Sources:

- *Biographies of Alaska-Yukon Pioneers, Volume II*. Ed Ferrell. Heritage Books. 1995,
- Correspondence with Debbie Currence, granddaughter of Robert Young. 2013
- *Early History of Thurston County, Washington*. Edited by Geogiana Blankenship. No publisher, Olympia, Washington.1914
- *Fairbanks, a City Historic Building Survey*. Janet Matheson. City of Fairbanks. 1985
- Fairbanks North Star Borough property records
- *Report of the Governor of the District of Alaska to the Secretary of the Interior*. U.S. Government Printing Office. 1901

Fairbanks - Pioneer Park, Gold Rush Town

Prostitute's crib at Pioneer Park Gold Rush Town

## Life on the Line in Fairbanks historic red light district

Economic depression gripped most of the western world during the 1890s. To escape their economic plight, an estimated 100,000 stampeders from all over the world raced north during the 1897-98 Klondike gold rush. The majority were men, but (since depressions are equal opportunity oppressors) a goodly percentage of women chanced the trip as well.

All were lured by adventure and the possibility of riches—however women were disadvantaged in finding fortune. Mining was essentially closed to them because of social mores and the physical strength required. Consequently, women were usually relegated to domestic work. A significant number of northbound women were prostitutes and professional entertainers though.

About 80 percent of the population in the Yukon and Alaska was male. Prostitution was viewed as a "necessary evil"—required to satisfy the needs of the predominantly male population and protect "respectable" women from potential abuse. In communities across the region, governments decided the best way to control prostitution was segregating the ladies in "restricted districts."

According to Lael Morgan's book, *Good Time Girls of the Alaska-Yukon Gold Rush*, Judge James Wickersham (who moved his court to Fairbanks in 1903) instituted a policy of "moderately taxing vice for civic betterment." Prostitutes and others on society's fringe, such as gamblers, were tolerated but required to pay monthly fines (essentially license fees) which helped support city government.

Because of this encouragement, and lax law enforcement, by 1906 Fairbanks was a rough-and-tumble town. Episcopal Archdeacon Hudson Stuck was dismayed by the frequent violence (often instigated by pimps and their ladies) but believed outlawing prostitution was unrealistic. His suggestion to the city council was a separate district for prostitutes, similar to one established at Dawson in 1899.

With city backing (if not official approval) the red light district, soon called the "Line" or "Row," was established at the edge of downtown, between Cushman and Barnette Streets along Third and Fourth Avenues. Prostitutes had to confine their services to the district, with no solicitation allowed elsewhere.

The district was regularly patrolled, and as long as the ladies paid their monthly "fines," they had no fear of police harassment. The prostitutes also agreed to routine health screenings. Within a few years the city also passed ordinances minimizing the role of pimps.

In 1908 a fence with gates was erected across both ends of the district to protect the sensitivities of respectable people. Not that much occurred outside. Prostitutes' more discreet activities were confined to their small cabins (called "cribs"). The 9' x 12' single-room log cabin in the drawing is one such crib. Now at Pioneer Park, it originally stood along Fourth Avenue. Cribs varied considerably. Some were multi-room frame structures. A few even had second stories with gable windows.

Most of the cribs actually faced inward—their living rooms with large picture windows and doors opening on to the alley between Third and Fourth Avenues. It was along the alley's boardwalk that men would go "window shopping." If a lady's window shades were open then her trade goods were available.

There was little trouble along the Line for most of its existence. Some contemporary writers spoke of the Northern ladies as a breed apart from prostitutes elsewhere. Judge Wickersham wrote that they were "of a more robust class than usual among their kind… less addicted to criminal activities outside of those peculiar to their mode of life."

The ladies of the Line were tolerated by respectable society (even if not allowed to actively mingle), and they were known to support local charities and grubstake prospectors. Patrons felt little fear that prostitutes would take more than their fair share of a miner's poke, and some miners even left valuables with their favorite ladies for safekeeping.

The Line survived almost 50 years, but was finally closed in 1952, not because of local opposition, but at the insistence of the federal government. Most of the cribs were demolished in the mid-1950s, eventually replaced by Safeway and Woolworth stores.

Sources:

- *Ghosts of the Gold Rush, a walking tour of Fairbanks*. Terrence Cole. Tanana-Yukon Historical Society. 1977
- *Good Time Girls of the Alaska-Yukon Gold Rush*. Lael Morgan. Epicenter Press. 1998
- *Old Yukon: Tales—Trails—Trials*. James Wickersham. Washington Law Book Company. 1938.
- Signage along Fourth Avenue. Fairbanks North Star Borough Historical Preservation Commission

Fairbanks - Pioneer Park, Gold Rush Town

Harding Car at Alaskaland (now Pioneer Park) in 1996

## Harding Car a part of Alaska Presidential history

Many Fairbankans have probably seen the "Denali" Pullman car on display at Pioneer Park, but how many actually know its history?

It was part of the Alaska Railroad's "Congressional Special" train that carried President Warren G. Harding and his entourage from Seward to Fairbanks and back in 1923. Harding was the first president to visit Alaska, and one of his primary purposes for the visit was to celebrate the completion of the Alaska Railroad by driving a golden spike at Nenana.

Most of the railroad had actually been completed by 1919. The missing link, however, was a bridge across the Tanana River. That took several years to complete, and until it was, passengers and freight were ferried across the Tanana between trains when the river was ice-free, and tracks were laid across the ice during the winter.

When the bridge was finally completed, President Harding drove a 14-carat golden spike into a railroad tie at the new bridge on July 15, 1923. (After the ceremonial spike was driven, it was removed and replaced by an iron spike. The golden spike is now in a private collection.)

Harding then continued on to Fairbanks to inspect the new Alaska Agricultural College and School of Mines. While in Fairbanks, President Harding stayed at the Pioneer Hotel, and also found time to address a gathering from the front steps of the Masonic Temple.

President Harding's train consisted of a locomotive and nine cars: a baggage car; business car; smoking car; sleeper cars "Fairbanks," "Talkeetna," "and "Anchorage"; dining car "McKinley Park"; and compartment-observation cars "Kenai" and "Denali." His entourage included 23 government officials and their wives, 32 members of the press, and 30 railroad employees.

The Pullman car which President Harding traveled in is commonly called the "Harding Car." Built in 1905, it is 10 feet wide and 81 feet long. As originally configured it had four staterooms, a drawing room, buffet room, card room, and observation room. It began service with the Great Northern Railway but was sold to the Alaska Railroad in 1923, which renamed it the "Denali."

The car was modified in 1928. In an article on the AlaskaRails.org website, Fairbanks railroad historian Pat Durand surmises that 1928 was when the observation room was expanded by removing the buffet and card rooms.

The car remained in passenger service until 1945 when it was converted into an "outfit car" (railroad employee housing). Later that same year it was retired to a siding in Nenana, where it sat for 14 years.

According to the National Register of Historic Places, in 1959 the Pioneers of Alaska, Igloo No. 4 in Fairbanks, asked the Alaska Railroad if the car could be moved to Fairbanks to use as a museum. The railroad refurbished the car in 1959-60 and then donated it to the City of Fairbanks.

It was brought to Fairbanks in 1965 and then relocated to its present site at Pioneer Park for the 1967 Alaska Purchase Centennial Celebration. (Pioneer Park was the A-67 site then.) Additional restoration work was completed after the car was installed at Pioneer Park. There has been some deterioration to the car's exterior since then, and in 2009 a protective canopy was built over it.

The car is quite handsome, with arched exterior windows and doors, leaded glass panels across the top of most of the windows, and elaborate exterior brass railings. The interior is just as ornate, with dark wood paneling on the walls, lighter wood paneling covering the arched ceiling, milk-glass and brass wall sconces and ceiling fixtures, and brass ornamentation—accoutrements usually not seen in modern times on government property used by the public.

Sources:

- "Alaska Railroad Passenger Cars, Car No. 3." from AlaskaRails.org website. 2013
- "Harding Railroad Car National Register of Historic Place Inventory-Nomination Form." Joan M. Antonson, National Park Service, 1977
- "Renovations continue on Pioneer Park's Harding car." Jeff Richardson. in *Fairbanks Daily News-Miner*. 9-10-2009
- "President Harding visits the New Alaska College in 1923." LaVern Keys. UA Journey. University of Alaska Fairbanks website, 2011

Fairbanks - Garden Island, N. Cushman Street

Big I Pub in the fall of 2013

## Big I Pub dispenses history as well as hospitality

Saloons and churches were both integral parts of frontier Alaska. Many early churches survive, while examples of early liquor establishments are rare. Perhaps this is because missionaries and preachers thought in terms of eternity and built their churches accordingly. Saloon owners on the other hand were thinking of immediate profits and for the most part weren't sure their establishments would last more than a few years—and built accordingly.

There were saloons along the riverfront in Fairbanks a least a year before churches were built. The first church services in Fairbanks were actually held in saloons by clergy visiting town.

The book, *Oh Ye Frost and Cold, a History of St. Matthews Church*, recounts that in March of 1903, the Reverend Charles Rice mushed from Circle City to Fairbanks to investigate the new mining camp. While in Fairbanks he held the town's first church service in a tent-frame saloon. The barkeep covered his bottles with a white cloth during worship, and the other saloon in town closed for the duration of the service.

The drawing shows the Big I Pub, located just north of the Cushman and Barnette Street bridges in the Garden Island area. Garden Island actually used to be an island, separated by a small slough (long-ago filled in) from the Tanana Mill Lumber Company site (later the Fairbanks Exploration Company complex, and now the Golden Valley Electric Association offices). Christian Heine, a Klondike veteran, named the island when he established a homestead there in 1903.

Garden Island was one of the areas that provided early Fairbanks with fresh produce. (The other was on the south edge of Fairbanks.) St. Joseph's Hospital, Immaculate Conception Church, businesses, warehouses, and the Tanana Mines Railroad quickly began claiming land there, and as Fairbanks expanded, the truck gardens and farms moved farther out of town.

Steamboat Slough (so-called because some steamboats overwintered in its protected waters) separated Garden Island from the larger land mass to the north. This small slough was located about where Phillips Field road is now. Long-time Fairbanks resident Jim Moody told me that the slough was gradually filled in, with much of the fill being clinkers from the Fairbanks Exploration Company power plant.

According to the Fairbanks North Star Borough's Commission on Historic Preservation, The Big I began life as the International Hotel and Bar, in a wood-frame building constructed by Emil Pozza in 1920. It was originally located approximately where the traffic island between the Cushman and Barnette Street bridges is now. However, in 1923 it and several other buildings were moved about 100 feet to the west across Turner Street to make room for the Cushman Street right-of-way and the new Alaska Railroad depot.

The hotel burned down in the 1940s, but Pozza rebuilt in 1950, this time erecting a two-story concrete-block and reinforced-concrete building with basement. The 29-foot by 100-foot building opened as the Big International Hotel and Bar. The bar was on the first floor, with hotel rooms on the floor above.

The Big International Hotel was forced to close after the 1967 Chena River Flood, but Jack Sexton bought and repaired the building, re-opening it in 1971 as the Big International Bar (usually shortened to just the Big "I"). Bert "Hap" Ryder later became the bar's manager.

John Jackovich bought the building in 2006 and continues to operate the Big I as a pub. It used to be flanked by several other historic structures, including Samson's Hardware and the old West Coast Grocery store building. However, the rest of the structures on the block were torn down to make way for the approach to the new Barnette Street bridge.

Jackovich, with a keen interest in historic preservation, successfully fought to save his pub from destruction. His plans (contingent on funding) include fixing up the property and turning the second floor into a venue for meetings and large social gatherings.

Sources:

- Conversation with Jim Moody, long-time Fairbanks resident. 2013
- Conversation with John Jackovich, owner. 2013
- Fairbanks North Star Borough Commission on Historic Preservation signage
- *Fairbanks, a City Historic Building Survey.* Janet Matheson. City of Fairbanks. 1985
- *Like a Tree to the Soil, a history of farming in Alaska's Tanana Valley, 1903-1940.* Josephine Papp & Josie Phillips. School of Natural Sciences and Agricultural Sciences, University of Alaska Fairbanks. 2007
- "Old Pioneer Laid to Rest." in *The Pathfinder*. November, 1921 (article about Christian Heine)
- *O Ye frost and Cold, a history of St. Matthew's Episcopal Church*. Arnold Griese and Ed Bigelow. St. Matthew's Episcopal Church. 1980

The Noyes House in the fall of 2012

## Street widening gives clearer view of historic Noyes House

For years the historic Noyes House at 407 Illinois Street was obscured by fencing and trees. One of the "benefits" of the recent Illinois Street widening project was the elimination of the fence and trees along Minnie Street, opening up a clearer view of this important piece of Fairbanks history.

The house was built some time before 1911 by Fred Noyes, who owned the Tanana Mill lumber company. According to Terrence Cole's report for the State DOT, Historic Resources of the Minnie Street Corridor, Noyes was a Michigan lumberman who joined the hordes headed for the Klondike in 1897. He operated a sawmill at Dawson City before moving on to Fairbanks in 1903.

It appears that after arriving in Fairbanks, he built a sawmill at the mouth of Noyes Slough (named after him). However, he soon re-located his mill farther along the slough, about where Golden Valley Electric Association has its offices.

The Tanana Mill became the largest lumber supplier in the Fairbanks area. Noyes was successful enough with his mill and other business interests to have a three-story wood-frame house built at the southeast corner of his property (now the corner of Illinois and Minnie Streets). According to captions on photos in the University of Alaska archives the house was called "Essinoye" by its owners. It was probably the first three-story house in Fairbanks, and one of the most impressive homes in early Fairbanks. (It lost its third story after a 1960s fire.)

The first floor (with parlor, dining room, library and kitchen) had nine-foot ceilings and wood-paneled walls. A large wrap-around colonnaded porch stretched along its south and east sides. The second floor contained four bedrooms and a bathroom, and the third floor featured a billiard room. The third floor was tucked under a steeply pitched gable roof with its west gable end facing Illinois Street and a large gable-fronted dormer facing south. Essinoye was filled with elaborate Victorian furniture and collectibles, and a 1955 Fairbanks Daily News-Miner article recollected that most of the furnishings were imported from Europe.

In 1925 the house was sold to the Fairbanks Exploration Company which initially used it to house visiting employees from U.S. Smelting, Refining and Mining Company (the FE Company's parent company).

It was remodeled in 1928 and turned into two apartments for company employees. Changes to the first floor during the remodel included adding a bathroom to the main section of the house and constructing an addition with two bedrooms and a bathroom at the northwest corner of the building. A kitchen was also installed on the second floor, and stairs were erected at the rear of the building for access to the second-floor apartment.

Up until World War II the Noyes House was used for FE Company employee housing, but the federal government closed down gold mining in 1942 as a "non-essential" wartime activity. The building was temporarily taken over by the U.S. military as part of the Lend-Lease program supplying aircraft to the Soviet Union, and housed the Soviet commander and his staff. A U.S. Army publication on the history of Ladd Field notes that the Soviet-occupied residence gained a reputation as "a big party place."

After the war the FE Company resumed gold mining, but by the 1950s was winding down its dredging operations. In 1959 it sold the Noyes House to local businessmen to use as a funeral home.

The building's interior was severely damaged in a 1961 fire. As a result, the third floor was torn down and replaced with a low-pitched gable roof. The other two floors were rebuilt, but all the original interior detailing was lost. Much of the exterior detailing of the first two floors was saved however, including the wrap-around porch, and the building still has historical significance.

A new funeral home was built next door in 1966, after which the Noyes House was used (again) as employee housing. It is still owned by the funeral home.

Sources:

- *Fairbanks, a City Historic Building Survey.* Janet Matheson. City of Fairbanks. 1985
- *Fairbanks, a Pictorial History.* Claus-M. Naske & Ludwig Rowinski. The Donning Company Publishers. 1981
- Fairbanks North Star Borough property records
- *Historic resources of the Minnie Street corridor: final report.* Terrence Cole. Alaska DOT. 1989
- "Illinois Street Historic District National Register of Historic Places Registration Form." Judith Bittner. National Park Service. 2001
- "Oldtimes Recalled During Festivity." in *Fairbanks Daily News-Miner.* July 22, 1955
- Photographs from the Fred Noyes Collection. University of Alaska Fairbanks, Archives
- *The World War II Heritage of Ladd Field, Fairbanks, Alaska,* "Chapter 7, Life at Ladd Field." Cathy Price. Center for Environmental Management of Military Lands. 2004

Fairbanks - Railroad Industrial Area, Charles Street

FE Company machine shop in the early 1990s

## Fairbanks Exploration Company machine shop kept dredges running

When you are in the resource development industry, the infrastructure to support your business needs to be in place before your operations begin. And if your operations are at the end of a 2,000-mile-long supply line, having local support facilities is essential.

So it was with the Fairbanks Exploration Company when it moved into the Fairbanks area in the 1920s. Besides the Alaska Railroad from Seward to Fairbanks, and Tanana Valley Railroad from Fairbanks to Chatanika, there was a rudimentary road system and not much else in the way of infrastructure.

Before its dredges were brought in, the FE Company had to develop the Davidson Ditch water system, construct a power plant and electrical distribution system, erect support camps, and build warehousing and repair facilities.

One of the first support facilities completed was its company machine shop, located off Charles Street behind the FE Company office building on Illinois Street. The machine shop (shown in the drawing) was completed in 1927.

According to Matthew Reckard's study, *The F.E. Company Industrial Site: Historic Resources and Preservation Potential*, the original portion of the machine shop (the first steel-frame structure in Interior Alaska) is a 64' x 136' single-story building with 20' ceilings in the central area.

A large garage addition (40' x 80') was added to the south in 1941, and an open storage shed was constructed on the western end of the original portion at a later date. The building has numerous large multi-pane wood sash windows and is sheathed with shiplap siding and corrugated metal (all original).

This facility was the best equipped machine shop in Fairbanks. It was the repair center for company vehicles and equipment that couldn't be fixed in the field, and for fabricating tools and parts.

A 1931 publication put out by the U.S. Smelting, Refining and Mining Company (FE Company's parent) bragged that, "In order to take care of repair work the company has provided very complete repair shops at Fairbanks. The machine shop contains tools of sufficient size to handle all parts of the dredges and power plant equipment."

The last FE Company dredges shut down in the 1960s, and the company's successor, Alaska Gold Company, sold off its assets in the early 1990s. Golden Valley Electric Cooperative bought most of the Illinois Street property, along with the FE Company's office building, but John and Ramona Reeves (who owned Gold Dredge No. 8 and other historic properties) bought the machine shop and the land it sits on.

The Reeves renamed the machine shop the Daniel F. Eagan Machine Shop. Talking with Eagan's son, Pete, I learned that Dan, who grew up at Meehan on Fairbanks Creek, worked at the FE Company for over 40 years as a mining engineer, machinist, and master mechanic.

The machine shop still contains most of its milling machines and other equipment, still in working condition. One of the large machining lathes was used to resurface the axles for Engine No. 1 at Pioneer Park when it was restored in the 1990s.

The truck depicted in the drawing is a 1937 Ford 1-ton panel truck and it was an actual FE Company vehicle, still sitting on the property when I took my reference photos. (There was also a 1948 Ford truck there.) I have a friend who used to be a mechanic for the FE Company and he said the company mostly operated Ford vehicles.

The shop, which is on the National Register of Historic Places, hasn't seen much use or many visitors in recent years, but it is still there. The building's first floor windows are boarded up now, but the machine shop is still filled with machines and memories, waiting to tell its story.

Sources:

- *AX-I-DENT-AX Employees Magazine*. U.S. Smelting, Refining and Mining Company. Volume 16, March 1931
- Conversation with Glenn Gibson, former mechanic at FE Company. 2012
- Conversation with Pete Eagan–Dan Eagan's son. 2012
- *Fairbanks, a City Historic Building Survey*. Janet Matheson. City of Fairbanks. 1985
- *History of Alaska Operations of Unites States Smelting, Refining and Mining Company*. John Boswell. Mineral Industries Research Laboratory, University of Alaska, Fairbanks. 1979
- "Illinois Street Historic District, National Register of Historic Places Registration Form." Robert Irwin. National Park Service. 2001
- *The F.E. Company Industrial Site: Historic Resources and Preservation Potential*. Matthew Reckard. University of Oregon, Master's Degree project. 1993

Fairbanks - Slaterville, Well Street

The Earl and Pat Cook house in Slaterville is seen as it looked in early spring 2016. The house was completed in 1940.

## Slaterville: from hayfields to housing developments

The development of the Slaterville area, on the north side of the Chena River across from downtown Fairbanks, started soon after the city was established. It is a residential area now, but began as one of the farms that sprouted up around the town's edge.

Jorgine Anderson, who moved to Fairbanks from the Klondike, was one of the first people to farm in the area. She staked an 87-acre homestead that encompassed most of the land between Illinois Street to the west, Noyes Slough to the east and north, and the Chena River to the south—from the mouth of Noyes Slough to the mouth of Garden Island Slough.

She and her husband, Eric, operated a truck garden from their homestead for many years, supplying fresh produce to Fairbanks residents. When Jorgine died in 1917 her homestead application lapsed. Charles Slater, who had been living in Fairbanks since 1905, picked up the homestead and expanded the Anderson's operation. Photographs in the

University of Alaska archives show his property from the Chena River to the far side of Noyes Slough (near present-day College Road), cleared of trees and filled with fields of hay and other crops.

As the population of Fairbanks grew, houses started encroaching into agricultural areas near town and the truck gardeners and farmers on the periphery of town ceased operations entirely or fled to more distant locations. When construction of what would become Ladd Field just east of Fairbanks began in 1939, pressure for additional housing increased significantly.

Charles Slater, who received patent to his homestead in the 1920s and had been farming his land for over 20 years, evidently regarded 1939 as an excellent time to get out of agriculture. He hired Lee Linck, who had grown up in Fairbanks, to subdivide the property.

Slater began by subdividing his land nearest the Chena River first and then worked his way north. According to Terrence Cole's report, *Historic Resources of the Minnie Street Corridor,* the first section of the subdivision, platted in the summer of 1939, consisted of 16 lots between Slater and Well Street. The section to the north of that, which included Minnie Street, was surveyed in the fall of 1939, and the section that included Charles Street, one block north of Minnie, was platted in 1940.

Many of Slaterville's streets are named after Slater's relatives. Minnie Street was christened in honor of his first wife. (Minnie is buried in Birch Hill Cemetery. Her grave is easily visible on the lower slope, enclosed by a white picket fence.) Slater's daughter, Betty, and second wife, Clara, were also honored with streets named after them.

Earl and Pat Cook were one of the first couples to build in the new subdivision. In a 1985 *Fairbanks Daily News-Miner* article the Cooks said friends were dismayed by their plans and asked why they were "moving so far out of town."

Terrence Cole's report states that the Cooks purchased a lot at the corner of Well and Betty Street (238 Well Street) in 1939 for $500.00, and built a small 1-1/2 story wood-frame cottage (shown in the drawing) with a gabled roof. The house cost $8,100.00.

They later added a large flat-roofed addition to the east which included a garage accessible from the rear of the house. They also built a dining room addition to the west.

Slaterville grew rapidly. According to the 1950 U.S. Census, with a population of 611 people, Slaterville was the largest of the residential areas mushrooming around Fairbanks.

The area was annexed into the City of Fairbanks in 1959. Due to the barrier formed by Noyes Slough it has retained much of its residential charm.

Sources:

- Albert Johnson Photo Collection, UAF Archives
- *Fairbanks, A city historic building Survey, 1985.* Janet Matheson. City of Fairbanks. 1985
- *Fairbanks, a pictorial history.* Claus-M. Naske & Ludwig J. Rowinski. Donning Company. 1981
- Fairbanks North Star Borough property records
- *Historic Resources of the Minnie Street Corridor.* Terrence Cole. Alaska Department of Transportation and Public Facilities. 1989
- U.S. Census for 1950

Fairbanks - Slaterville, Well Street

The old Birch Hill ski cabin, now on Well Street in Fairbanks

## Skiing at Birch Hill in Fairbanks dates back to the 1930s

With skiing's long history in Nordic countries, it is not surprising the Swedes, Norwegians, Danes and Finns entering Alaska at the turn of the 20th century brought their skiing traditions with them. According to Elizabeth Tower's book, Skiing in Alaska, the 1899 Nome Gold Rush brought hundreds of Nordic prospectors (and their skis) to the Seward Peninsula. Cross-country skiing and ski jumping became popular winter recreation there. Leonhard Seppala, who later re-located to the Fairbanks area, was one of Nome's early ski jumping champions

After Seward Peninsula gold fever died down, many Nordic gold-seekers settled in Fairbanks. Skiing events were held sporadically, but the sport did not take off until the 1930s.

Tower states that part of skiing's rising popularity in Fairbanks was because of the arrival of Ivar Skarland at the Alaska Agricultural College and School of Mines in 1931.

Skarland, originally from Norway, came to the college as a student. He later went on to become a professor at the University of Alaska. An excellent skier, he taught fellow students the sport and helped develop ski trails on campus.

Another factor was the 1932 Winter Olympic Games held at Lake Placid, New York. The first Winter Olympics held in North America, it helped popularize winter sports across the nation.

*Fairbanks Daily News-Miner* articles from the early 1930s mention ski races from downtown Fairbanks to the college and back during the annual Fairbanks Ice Festival. At some point in the mid-1930s, however, the Ice Festival race course changed, making Birch Hill the mid-way point.

This probably coincided with the organization of the Fairbanks Ski Club in the winter 1935-36, with Leonhard Seppala as its first president. The club blazed ski trails on 10 acres of gentle slope on the southwestern edge of Birch Hill and erected a 24-foot by 24-foot ski hut constructed of round logs with saddle-notched corners, topped with a steeply-pitched hipped roof. A 1930s photograph shows the cabin with about two-dozen pairs of skis stuck in the snow outside.

By winter 1936-37, skiers were avidly ski jumping and traversing trails at Birch Hill. A Feb. 1, 1937, editorial in the News-Miner boasted of 250 skiers who had frolicked at Birch Hill the day before.

Those early Birch Hill trails were located on what used to be the northeast corner of Melvin Sabin's homestead. Melvin died in 1930, and Tony Zimmerman bought 47 acres of the former homestead (including the ski area) in 1937—transforming it into Birch Hill Cemetery a year later.

Zimmerman acknowledged that the ski trails and cabin would have to move. However, he planned to move the cabin to a nearby location and said there was plenty of room to the east for ski trails.

The ski trails did indeed move eastward — to sections of Birch Hill that eventually became part of Fort Wainwright. Many of the new trails were cut by volunteers while others were cut by Civilian Conservation Corps crews. A rope-tow and ski jump were also constructed. Some of the original ski trails are now part of the Fairbanks North Star Borough's Birch Hill Recreation Area.

The ski club's cabin was still at Birch Hill in 1939, but according to Terrence Cole's book Historic Resources of the Minnie Street Corridor, Joe Reynolds then moved it to its present location at the east end of Well Street in Slaterville, next to Noyes Slough. In 1942 or '43 Ted and Alberta Matthews bought the cabin, adding a 14-foot by 24-foot two-bedroom addition to the left side of the structure. The addition and changes to the roof mirrored the original construction.

The cabin has remained virtually unchanged since then.

The cabin was owned for a time by Chugach School District, which also owned the two-story building next to it. The old cabin is once again a private residence. With wooded borough property behind it, it's like having a little bit of Birch Hill in downtown Fairbanks

Sources:

- "Birch Hill Ski Jump." From Alaska Lost Ski Areas Project website. No date
- *Fairbanks Daily News-Miner* articles – 1933, 1934,1937, 1938, 1939, 1940
- Fairbanks North Star Borough property records
- *Historic Resources of the Minnie Street Corridor*. Terrence Cole. Alaska Department of Transportation and Public Facilities. 1989
- "Skiing in Fairbanks, 1937." Jim Ducker. Alaska Historical Society webpage. No date
- *Umbrella Guide to Skiing in Alaska, Downhill & Cross-country*. Elizabeth Tower. Epicenter Press. 1997

Fairbanks - Slaterville, Charles Street

The Stepovich house at 323 Charles St. was once the residence of Territorial Gov. Mike Stepovich.

## Alaska's last territorial governor, Mike Stepovich, called Fairbanks home

Michael (Mike) Anthony Stepovich, was Alaska's last Territorial Governor, shepherding the territory through one of its most pivotal periods, the fight for Statehood.

Mike's father was Marko "Wise Mike" Stepovich, an immigrant from Montenegro who joined the Klondike Gold Rush in 1897. (The Alaska Mining Hall of Fame relates that Wise Mike got his moniker by outfoxing some of Soapy Smith's con men in Southeast Alaska. Others say the nickname came from the Montenegrin's wise-cracking nature.)

Wise Mike moved to Fairbanks from the Klondike in the fall of 1902. By the end of the 1910s he had secured financial success mining tungsten and gold in the Gilmore Dome and Fairbanks Creek areas. In 1918 he married another Balkan immigrant, Olga Barta, who had been living in the Portland, Oregon area.

Wise Mike moved his bride into his Fairbanks Creek cabin, and in 1919 their son, Mike, was born at St. Joseph's hospital. Olga had already decided frontier life did not suit her and after Mike's birth she bundled him up and moved back to Portland, eventually divorcing Wise Mike and remarrying.

Wise Mike kept in touch though, and in 1937 Mike, who was in college, began spending his summers in Alaska working for his father. After graduating from Gonzaga University in 1941 Mike went on to earn a law degree from Notre Dame in 1943.

Mike then enlisted in the Navy, serving in its legal department during World War II. After his discharge in 1947 Mike headed back to Alaska, making a brief stop in the Portland area to court and marry Matilda Baricevic, who was living in the Balkan community there. The two arrived in Fairbanks in late 1947, moving into an apartment house that had been owned by Wise Mike (who died in 1944).

Mike went into private practice in Fairbanks, but also worked as the city attorney. In 1948 he and Matilda bought the house shown in the drawing, located at 323 Charles Street, one block north of Minnie Street. The 30' x 34' 1 ½-story wood-frame house, with its steeply pitched roof and simple lines, was constructed in about 1946 or 1947 for a Mr. Cantrell, who was an employee of the Northern Commercial Company.

According to Terrence Cole's 1989 report, *Historic Resources of the Minnie Street Corridor,* the house as originally constructed was a mirror image of the house next door at 319 Charles Street. It has been extensively modified since then, though. When Mike and Matilda moved in, the house only had two bedrooms, but the Stepovichs ended up raising 13 children there. Over time they added three bedrooms in the basement, plus building a 20' x 27' addition to the rear of the house with three more bedrooms upstairs.

In 1950 Mike was elected to the Territorial House of Representatives and two years later moved to the Territorial Senate. In 1957 he was appointed Territorial Governor by President Dwight D. Eisenhower.

Stepovich worked his way out of the governorship by tirelessly laboring for Alaska Statehood. He crisscrossed the United States lobbying for statehood, even appearing on an episode of the television show, "What's My Line.'

On June 30, 1958 Congress passed the Alaska Statehood Bill, and President Eisenhower signed it on July 7. A month later, with special elections planned to select new State officers, Stepovich resigned as Territorial governor.

Mike was unsuccessful in his subsequent campaigns for elected office and returned to private practice in Fairbanks. Throughout all this time he and Matilda maintained the house on Charles Street as their legal residence. They moved to Medford, Oregon in 1978. The Charles Street house is now owned by Mike's son, Christopher.

Matilda passed away in 2003. Mike died in 2014 and was buried beside his wife at Birch Hill Cemetery.

Sources:

- Fairbanks North Star Borough property records
- "Gov. Mike Stepovich," obituary. In *Fairbanks Daily News-Miner*. 2-16-2014
- *Historic Resources of the Minnie Street Corridor*. Terrence M. Cole. Alaska Department of Transportation and Public Facilities. 1989
- "Wise' Mike Stepovich." Thomas K. Bundtzen. Alaska Mining Hall of Fame Foundation. 2015

Fairbanks - Slaterville, Minnie Street

The old Northside Grocery building on Minnie Street had the first self-serve gas pumps in Fairbanks.

## Slaterville comes of age, complete with gas pumps

After 1939, when construction began at Ladd Field, and well into 1950s, Fairbanks experienced a population explosion. Terrence Cole's report, *Historic Resources of the Minnie Street Corridor*, states that between 1939 and 1950 the area's population increased by 240 percent, and between 1950 and 1953 the population doubled to about 31,000 people.

Residential areas developed around the city's edges, including Slaterville, north of the Chena River and across from downtown Fairbanks. The city's burgeoning population, along with military activities and renewed mineral extraction in the area, severely taxed the area's transportation system. The Minnie Street Bridge across Noyes Slough, along with the Wendell Street Bridge across the Chena River, were constructed in 1953 as part of the city's efforts to modernize its outdated road system.

The only bridge across the Chena River before completion of the Wendell Street Bridge was the Cushman Street

Bridge, built in 1917. The old two-lane steel-truss Cushman bridge was narrow, allowing only passenger vehicles to pass each other. Busses and trucks had to straddle the bridge's central beam to cross.

The Minnie Street and Wendell Street bridges diverted traffic from Cushman Street. When completed, they became part of the first intentionally-designed truck route through an Alaskan city.

One of the most recognizable landmarks along Minnie Street is the old concrete-block Northside Grocery. Located at 140 Minnie Street, it was, according to Cole's report, built in 1952 by long-time Fairbanks resident, Carl Heflinger, in anticipation of the opening of the new bridges.

Heflinger was better-known as a miner than a merchant. Coming to Fairbanks in 1934, Carl worked as a drift and open-cut miner until World War II intervened and he joined the Army.

Stationed at Ladd Field during the war, he met and married Dorothy Brady and they built a home in the expanding Slaterville subdivision.

After the war Dorothy convinced Carl to get a "real" job rather than return to mining. He went to work for Mitchell Truck and Tractor as a mechanic and eventually helped form GHEMM contacting. It was also during this period that he and his wife decided to put up a new building at the corner of Minnie and Clara Streets next to their house.

According to Carl's son, Dave, the gas station was more of an afterthought that a calculated plan. Carl and Dorothy wanted to build an apartment house. However, a friend suggested cutting the corner off the building at the Minnie and Clara intersection so that gas pumps could be installed, and Carl decided that was an excellent idea.

Dave told me that his mother often rued the change in plans, saying it would have been much easier running just an apartment house. However, Carl, having fueled aircraft during the war, and worked as a mechanic afterwards, thought running a service station made sense. In addition to selling gas, he operated a towing business and repaired vehicles in a garage at the back of the building.

The Heflinger's also rented out apartments in the basement and on the first floor, and later added a small grocery to the operation.

Carl eventually tired of city work and returned to mining in 1958, but he and Dorothy owned the grocery and gas station until the 1980s. After Carl left the day-to-day operation of the business, the ground under the garage was excavated and more basement apartments added, as well as the garage itself being converted into apartments. The grocery, which had occupied a tiny corner of the building, also expanded.

The service station and grocery eventually closed. For a period the building was used as a religious outreach center, but has now reverted to its original purpose as an apartment house.

Sources:

- Carl Heflinger obituary. Fairbanks Daily News-Miner. 12-30-2014
- Carl Heflinger presentation to the Pioneers of Alaska on 4-17-2000. Oral History Collection at the University of Alaska Fairbanks
- Conversation with Dave Heflinger, one of Carl's and Dorothy's sons
- "Historic Resources of the Minnie Street Corridor." Terrence Cole. Alaska Department of Transportation and Public Facilities. 1989
- Property records at the Fairbanks North Star Borough

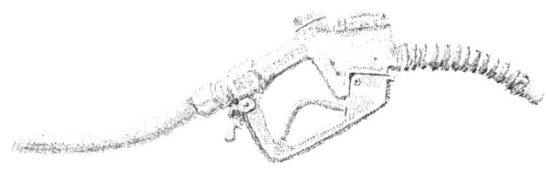

Fairbanks - Graehl, Front Street

This old cabin at 624 Front St. in Graehl is one of the oldest surviving residences in Fairbanks' first suburb.

## Despite commercialization, homes can still be found in Graehl, Fairbanks' first suburb

Fairbanks has 2nd, 3rd and 4th Avenues on the south side of the Chena River, and on the north are 2nd, 3rd and 4th Streets? Why does Fairbanks have such a confusing duplication of names?

Actually, there was no duplication before Graehl, on the north side of the Chena River, was incorporated into the City of Fairbanks. Prior to its annexation Graehl was a stubbornly separate little community.

Graehl, on the Chena River's north bank upstream from the eastern end of Noyes Slough and west of Hamilton Acres subdivision, could be considered Fairbanks' first suburb.

Michael Carey, who grew up there, wrote in a 2013 article in the *Alaska Dispatch News* that when he lived in Graehl, it was a community of "small cabins, tarpaper shacks and modest frame houses." Before becoming part of

Fairbanks it was a fiercely independent little burgh with a history going back almost as far as Fairbanks itself.

The un-ceremonious offloading of E.T. Barnette, his entourage and trade goods in 1901 on the south bank of the Chena River marked the beginning of Fairbanks. The Chena River's bank was not Barnette's desired location but circumstances forced him to establish his trading post there.

A promise of gold in nearby creeks convinced Barnette to stay put, but big strikes didn't occur until 1903. By that time several other towns had sprung up around Fairbanks. These included Chena at the mouth of the Chena River, and Graehl, just upstream from Fairbanks on the opposite side of the river.

Graehl was laid out in 1903 by Hyrum Graehl, an early gold seeker who evidently saw more profit in selling lots than mining. Hyrum had come north to the Klondike from Utah in 1898 and eventually found his way to the Tanana Valley. Carey also wrote in his article that Hyrum "was so much the gold rush progeny that streets were named for mining camps - Rampart, Circle, Dawson, Eagle, Fortymile." Hyrum eventually returned to Utah and died there in 1952 at the age of 89.

According to Terrence Cole's report, *Historic Resources of the Minnie Street Corridor*, the people attracted to Graehl in the early 1900s either couldn't afford to live in Fairbanks proper, or were simply indifferent to life south of the river. During its early years it was mostly populated by bachelor prospectors and Native families.

At first Graehl was connected to Fairbanks by a ferry that crossed the Chena about where the Wendell Street Bridge is now. Later, the Alaska Road Commission built two bridges (in succession) across Noyes Slough connecting Slater Street (and the Cushman Street Bridge) on the slough's west side with Front Street on the east side. Early maps show this route as part of the "Fairbanks-Fox Wagon Road."

When the Wendell Street Bridge across the Chena River and Minnie Street Bridge across Noyes Slough were completed in 1953 the bridge between Slater and Front Streets was torn down.

Cole also writes in his report that until the 1960s, Graehl "was largely a community of little log cabins and big junkyards, with almost as many dogs as people, and the people were stubbornly independent." Graehl's residents showed a disdain for local government and taxes, doing for themselves what was necessary, or taking up collections to maintain streets and other improvements. It was only after a bitter struggle during the 1960s that most of Graehl was annexed into the city of Fairbanks in 1970.

The nature of Graehl has gradually changed from residential and rural (Charles and Belle Hinckley once operated a dairy there) to commercial. This process started with completion of the Wendell and Minnie Street bridges and accelerated as major arterial roads developed, crisscrossing the area. The first mall in Fairbanks, Gavora Mall, was built along Graehl's Third Street in the 1960s.

With the 1970s completion of the Steese Expressway, Graehl split in two. West of the expressway it lost its residential nature. To the east, beyond a patch of commercial development, is a remnant of old Graehl, with log cabins and frame houses, and even a few junk yards. The log cabin shown in the drawing, built in about 1920 and one of the oldest houses in Graehl, is located there, at 624 Front Street.

Sources:

- *Fairbanks, a Gold Rush Town that Beat the Odds*. Dermot Cole. University of Alaska Press. 1999
- Fairbanks North Star Borough property records
- "Family Ties to Felix Pedro cover a lot of miles." *What's His Name*. In *Fairbanks Daily News Miner*
- *Historic Resources of the Minnie Street Corridor*. Terrence Cole. Alaska Department of Transportation. 1989
- "The Garage in Graehl was a trove of treasure." Michael Carey. In *Alaska Digital News*. 11-15-2015

Fairbanks - College Road, Fountainhead Antique Auto Museum

Tom Gibson's 1916 Dodge Model 30-35 touring car as it looks today

# The early Richardson Highway and the Gibson Stage Line

The Richardson Highway stretches 368 miles from Valdez on Prince William Sound to Fairbanks in the Tanana River Valley. In its earliest form—the Valdez-Fairbanks Trail—it was the dominant overland route into Interior Alaska.

The Valdez-Fairbanks Trail also was called the Richardson Trail, named after Major Wilds P. Richardson, the first president of the Alaska Road Commission (ARC). The trail was blazed in about 1903 as an offshoot of the Valdez-Eagle Trail.

After the ARC formed in 1905, improvement of the Richardson Trail became a priority. By 1910 it had been upgraded to an all-season wagon road (albeit a very primitive wagon road in places).

A few automobiles had already appeared in Fairbanks (freighted in on steamboats), and as the Richardson's road conditions improved, adventurers began testing their vehicles against it. By 1909 autos could be driven as far as Birch Lake about 60 miles southeast of Fairbanks. According to the book, *The Trail, the Story of the Historic Valdez-Fairbanks Trail,* some entrepreneurs teamed up with stage lines to take passengers part-way to-and-from Valdez via motor vehicles.

By 1912 road conditions improved enough that some dared think it might be possible to drive all the way between Fairbanks and Valdez. All the major streams and rivers except five had been bridged, and those five had ferry service across them.

Bobby Sheldon of Fairbanks was the first to succeed in driving the Richardson. He had been interested in motor vehicles even as a youth. While living is Skagway in 1905 he built the first automobile in Alaska. (That home-built vehicle is on display at the University of Alaska Museum of the North.)

In early 1913 he ordered a Ford Model T from Samson's Hardware. It wasn't long after its arrival in June that Bobby began toying with the idea of driving the car from Fairbanks to Chitina (and the Copper River and Northwestern Railroad) and then on to Valdez. With two burly passengers (who helped pull the little flivver out of mud holes and across flooded streams) Bobby made the groundbreaking trip between July 29 and Aug. 2.

His wasn't the only vehicle to successfully make the trip that year, though. The ARC sent a truck out from Valdez on July 28 loaded with supplies for camps along the trail. It accomplished the same feat in a slightly longer time, arriving in Fairbanks on Aug. 6.

With motor vehicles having finally conquered the trail, auto usage picked up. In 1914 Bobby started an auto stage line, partnering with another Fairbanksan, Tom Gibson. The next year Gibson started his own line, "Gibson Auto Stage."

Gibson started running a few Fords like Sheldon, but soon concentrated on Dodges. According to a 1958 *Fairbanks Daily News-Miner* article, Gibson operated 23 vehicles, such as the 1916 Dodge Model 30-35 touring car shown in the drawing.

The Dodge, now owned by David Stone and Don and Ray Cameron and on loan to the Fountainhead Antique Auto Museum, was modified by Gibson for his business's special needs. The fuel tank was originally at the back of the vehicle, but in order to make more room for luggage the tank was repositioned under the front seat. The frame was jacked up several inches, and a metal support bar was installed between the front fenders to keep them from rattling.

The Valdez-Fairbanks Trail was officially designated the Richardson Road in 1919. Between 1920 and 1927 the road was gradually improved to automobile standards, eventually becoming the Richardson Highway.

With the completion of the Glenn Highway in 1945 (linking Southcentral with the Interior's road system) the Richardson became a conduit for drivers traveling between Anchorage and Fairbanks. Construction of the Parks Highway in the 1970s reduced traffic on the Richardson, but recent improvements to the Glenn and Richardson Highways have brought a resurgence in travel along the scenic roadway.

Sources:

- "Gibson ran early-day stage." in *Fairbanks Daily News-Miner.* 7-18-1958
- "History of the Valdez Trail." Geoffrey Bleakley. from Wrangell-St. Elias National Park and Preserve web site. 2013
- "Major Roads of Alaska." National Park Service. 1944
- Signage at Fountainhead Antique Auto Museum
- *The Trail, the Story of the Historic Valdez-Fairbanks Trail.* Kenneth Marsh. Trapper Creek Museum. 2008

Fairbanks - Lemeta, O'Connor Road

A 1947 cabin standing in Lemeta, which was one of the first housing developments built in Fairbanks after World War II.

# Lemeta is an eclectic mix of rustic cabins and modern homes

The late 1940s through the 1950s were a tumultuous period for Fairbanks. Mining, the mainstay of the Fairbanks economy before World War II, was finally rebounding from its wartime lull, attracting new residents.

Military personnel and civilians associated with the military also poured into the area at a frenetic pace as the Cold War with the Soviet Union heated up and the U.S. federal government consequently expanded its presence to counter Soviet activities.

The supply of housing in Fairbanks proved sorely inadequate, with demand outstripping supply. New housing developments went up at a swift pace, but spare bedrooms and church fellowship halls were routinely pressed into serviced to temporarily house new residents.

In addition to developments such as Slaterville and Rickert Subdivision, which came into existence immediately before World War II and continued to fill up after the war, apartment complexes such as the Northward Building were constructed, and new residential developments began popping up around the periphery of the city.

According to a 1986 City of Fairbanks report, "Historic Districts in the City of Fairbanks." 20 subdivisions were developed in the Fairbanks area between 1944 and 1960. Subdivisions opened during this period included, Hamilton Acres, Westgate, Taku, and Aurora.

Lemeta subdivision was also developed after World War II. The Lemeta area, located between Noyes Slough and Creamers Field along College Road, was originally a homestead that John and Bridget O'Connor filed for on August 14, 1923.

College Road, then called College Highway, ran across the O'Connor homestead. The road originated as part of the trail from Fairbanks to Ester. After the Alaska College of Agriculture and School of Mines was established in 1917, the trail from the college into Fairbanks was gradually upgraded.

John O'Connor died before receiving title to the homestead, but on May 5, 1930, Bridget received patent to 103.53 acres.

According to a 1985 interview of Bud Meyeres by Gayle Malloy, Meyeres, along with his partners, Warren Taylor and Girdelle Lee, bought the homestead sometime in the early 1940s and developed it into a subdivision. The name Lemeta is a combination of the first two letters of each partner's last name. (The partnership went on to develop other housing developments such as Westgate and McKinley subdivisions.)

The survey for the Lemeta subdivision is dated October 13, 1948. However, Borough records indicate that numerous residences in the area were built before that date.

It is probable that as soon as Meyeres and partners began laying out streets, would-be home-owners lined up to buy lots.

Many of the subdivision streets were named after friends and relatives. The street running along Noyes Slough is O'Connor Road, and an intersecting street is named Bridget. A 1949 aerial photo shows the present street layout, with a smattering of development. Lemeta continued to mature during the 1950s and 60s.

Most of the early homes in Lemeta were small. The gable-roofed log cabin shown in the drawing is typical of early structures. The cabin is located at 929 O'Connor Road—on the bank of Noyes Slough, and was constructed in about 1947. The front part of the cabin, which is the original structure, is only 17' x 21'. A bathroom and bedroom addition, also of logs, was added to the rear later.

Lemeta has changed gradually. Many homes have expanded—some with so many additions that the original building is lost from sight. Modern houses have replaced others. But Lemeta remains true to its roots, an eclectic mix of rustic cabins, modern homes, and back yards filled with memories of how Fairbanks used to be.

Sources:

- "Bud Mcyeres is interviewed by Gayle Malloy on September 27, 1985." University of Alaska Oral History Collection
- *Fairbanks, A city historic building survey, 1985.* Janet Matheson. City of Fairbanks. 1985
- "Fairbanks, Alaska: A Survey of Progress." Richard. A Cooley. Alaska Development Board. July, 1954
- Fairbanks North Star Borough property records
- "Historic Districts in the City of Fairbanks." Janet Matheson. City of Fairbanks. September 1986
- "Lemeta Subdivision: Survey of Bridget O'Connor Homestead." At City of Fairbanks Engineering Department. Dated Oct. 13, 1948

Fairbanks - College Road, Creamers Field

Case L tractor in front of creamery at Creamers Dairy

## The early years of Creamers Dairy

When Charles and Belle Hinckley arrived in Fairbanks in the spring of 1904, they had no inkling that they would establish what would become a bird sanctuary 70 years later. They were just searching for their personal bonanza—not by mining gold, but by milking cows.

The Hinckleys (originally from Washington state) heard of Nome's strike in 1900, but instead of sailing north with shovels and gold pans, they sailed with several Holstein milk cows. Charles and Belle ran a successful dairy in the Nome area until the gold strike began petering out.

Then, hearing of new opportunities in Interior Alaska along the Chena River, they packed up their cows and took the first steamboat of the 1904 season from St. Michael on the Norton Sound coast up the Yukon, Tanana, and Chena Rivers to Fairbanks. It took 27 days to reach Fairbanks from St. Michael, during which time they helped pay for their passage by keeping passengers and crew supplied with fresh milk.

Charles and Belle originally ran a small dairy near Fourth and Kellum Street (what is now downtown). however, they eventually moved across the river to Graehl, a tiny community east of Noyes Slough.

Terrence Cole, in a report entitled, *Historic Resources of the Minnie Street Corridor,* states that Graehl, sometimes referred to as "North Fairbanks," could be considered the city's first suburb. There used to be a ferry between Fairbanks and Graehl where the Wendell Street Bridge now crosses the river.

The Hinckleys built a new log barn and house in Graehl. According to the book, *The History of Creamer's Dairy,* during this period the Hinckleys couldn't afford regular milk bottles, so they sterilized wine bottles and used them instead.

They soon were able to buy a 327 acre homestead three miles farther out of town, along what is now College Road. For several years, while they cleared additional land, the Hinckleys herded their cows to the homestead to graze in the summer and back to the barn in Graehl during the winter.

Eventually they moved their entire operation, including house. The structure was disassembled and the pieces carefully labeled before being hauled and re-assembled at the new site. The log house (the dairy's present farmhouse) was enlarged over the years and eventually covered with board and batten siding.

Belle's sister, Anne; and Anne's husband, Charles Creamer (who had grown up in Fairbanks); bought the dairy from the Hinckleys in 1928. They expanded the operation and in 1935 bought their first tractor, the Case L tractor shown in the drawing.

Switching from horse-drawn machinery to powered equipment was sometimes trying. According to Don Creamer (Charles Creamer's son) the tractor "had a habit of getting itself stuck," and needed to be pulled out with the old reliable horse team.

The Creamers eventually retired the Case and bought newer tractors, but hung on to the old tractor. It was restored by Robert and Barbara Moore and still has a home at the dairy.

In 1938 the Creamers had the largest and most modern barn in Alaska built for their operation. The new barn was 110 feet long, and 36 feet wide, with a huge hay loft capable of holding enough hay to get a 55-cow herd through a Fairbanks winter. To celebrate its completion, they held a barn dance with an estimated 1,000 people in attendance. In 1950 a second barn, nearly as big as the first, was constructed.

At the height of operations, the dairy employed between 12 and 16 people. It produced 250 to 300 gallons of milk and dairy products, and 400 to 600 gallons of ice cream and sherbet daily.

Unfortunately, changing market conditions and new health regulations eventually led to the dairy's demise. The Creamers were forced to close their dairy in 1966, but with support from the Fairbanks community it was brought back to life as Creamer's Field Migratory Waterfowl Refuge.

Sources:

- *A Place for the Birds, The Legacy of Creamer's Field Migratory Waterfowl Refuge.* Jessica A. Ryan. University of Alaska Fairbanks, Masters Thesis. 2003
- "Creamer's Dairy, National Register of Historic Places Nomination Form. Alfred Mongin. National Park Service. 1975
- *Historic Resources of the Minnie Street Corridor.* Terrence Cole. Alaska Department of Transportation and Public Facilities. 1980
- *The History of Creamer's Dairy.* Robin Lewis. Tanana-Yukon Historical Society. no date (1989)

Fairbanks - College Road, Tanana Valley State Fairgrounds

Badger Hall at the Tanana Valley State Fairgrounds is seen as it looks today.

## Tanana Valley State Fair a long-time tradition in Fairbanks

The state fair in Fairbanks is the oldest event of its kind in Alaska. Almost since its inception Fairbanks residents have touted the region's agricultural potential. One of the area's earliest agricultural boosters was Falcon Joslin, builder of the Tanana Valley railroad. (Of course, Joslin's main interest was boosting business for his railroad.)

Annual fairs in Fairbanks were preceded by periodic agricultural exhibits held at various locations around town. According to a 1974 article in the *All-Alaska Weekly* newspaper, one of the first exhibits was held in 1904. In 1907 a new building at 204 Wickersham Street, called "The Auditorium," became the site for these periodic exhibitions. The building was later the Moose Hall.

Between 1911 and 1924 agricultural exhibits were held at a roller rink in downtown Fairbanks. The event moved back to Moose Hall in 1924 and later to Main School.

In its early days the event was mainly an agricultural exposition. However, it quickly grew from just a venue showcasing grains and vegetables into an event including exhibits of preserved and processed foodstuffs, handiworks, and other items. The event has gone by numerous names including "The Annual Harvest Fair of the North," "Our Punkin Show," and "The County Fair." (This was before Statehood and the organizing of regions into "boroughs" rather than counties.)

Locals were not the only people interested in Alaska agriculture, either. The book, *Like a Tree to the Soil, a History of Farming in Alaska's Tanana Valley*, states that in the summer of 1917 West Coast businessmen visited Fairbanks to check out Interior Alaska's agriculture. In October of the same year the Tanana Valley Agriculture Association shipped an agricultural display to Seattle for the city's Northwest Land Products Exposition.

In 1924, a group of Fairbanks residents organized the non-profit Tanana Valley Fair Association (TVFA). The group was spearheaded by George Grasser (director of the Fairbanks agricultural experiment station) and Harry Badger (Fairbanks businessman and pioneer homesteader.) Under the TVFA's leadership the fair became a much more organized event. However, it still did not have a permanent home and was still a sporadically-held event. The fair was not held during the Great Depression, World War II, or in 1951.

On March 22, 1952 a group of people met to hopefully re-establish and revitalize the fair. One of the group's priorities was finding a permanent home for the fair. The newly revitalized fair association was able to complete a lease agreement with the University of Alaska for 40 acres, and that summer the fair moved to its present location off College Road.

The inaugural fair at the new location was dedicated to George Gasser and Harry Badger. One of the first buildings constructed at the fairgrounds was Badger Hall (named in honor of Harry) which is shown in the drawing.

## Fairbanks - College Road, Tanana Valley State Fairgrounds

This 40' x 120' 1 ½-story timber-frame structure, located at the fair's western end just north of a small slough, was originally the fair's horse barn. Horses were stabled on the ground floor, and people-centered activities were held on the second floor. (I don't think the stairs were wide enough to get horse up anyway.) On the ground floor you can still see the heavy timbers supporting the ceiling, and the timbers embedded in the north wall that divided the barn into stalls.

When new barns were constructed in 1981 Badger Hall was converted into exhibit space. While most activities in the building occur during the summer, Badger Hall is also available for use during the rest of the year.

Fair manager, Joyce Whitehorn, told me that even when the building appears "empty," it really isn't. "Johnny," one of the fair's resident ghosts, purportedly lives on the second floor and you can hear his is footsteps on the back stairs.

The fair has expanded to cover 100 acres, and now hosts activities throughout the year.

Sources:

- Conversation and correspondence with Joyce Whitehorn, Tanana Valley State Fair general manager
- "History reveals Tanana Valley Fair is community event." Vicki Oliver. "All-Alaska Weekly." Vol. 5, No. 5, August 9, 1974
- "Like a Tree to the Soil, a History of Farming in Alaska's Tanana Valley, 1903 to 1940." Josephine E. Papp & Josie A. Phillips. School of Natural Resources & Agricultural Sciences, University of Alaska. 2007
- "Seventy-six Years of Fair History." Stewart Rothman. h "This Month in Fairbanks," Vol. 7, No. 3. August 1980.
- "Tanana Valley State Fair and Fairground's Development Plan." Tanana Valley State Fair Association. March, 1981

Fairbanks - Birch Hill

Minnie Slater's grave at Birch Hill Cemetery in 2010

# Birch Hill Cemetery established to honor a wife's final wish

Antone "Tony" Zimmerman was a well-known miner in early Fairbanks. He is perhaps best-known, however, for developing and donating Birch Hill Cemetery to the Fairbanks community in the late 1930s.

Clay Street Cemetery in Fairbanks was beginning to fill up, but Zimmerman's motive for starting the facility at Birch Hill was in large part due to the wishes of his first wife, Serina. Before she died in 1938 Serina expressed her desire to be buried there.

Zimmerman, who owned 47 acres at the base of the hill fronting on Lazelle Road and the Steese Highway, interred her in a reinforced concrete crypt on a rocky outcropping overlooking Lazelle road. (Tony and his second wife, Ester, would later be buried beside Serina.)

Zimmerman's intention was to develop the entire 47 acres as a cemetery. According to an article in the November 8, 1938 issue of the *Alaska Miner* newspaper, the original Birch Hill ski area and cabin were located on the upper part of the tract. Zimmerman planned to relocate the cabin and ski area, building a mausoleum at their location. The cabin was moved, but the mausoleum never materialized.

Zimmerman cleared part of the hillside, and put in a road and drainage ditches. He also offered to "donate a plot free of charge to every church and lodge in Fairbanks that might desire the same, and the balance to the City of Fairbanks or to the general public, also free of charge." A 1938 plat of the land shows cemetery sections for most of Fairbanks's civic groups.

The Birch Hill Cemetery Association was formed to administer the new cemetery, but debate about the suitability of the land for a cemetery slowed its transfer. Some residents cited erosion problems with spring run-off, and the fact that no water was available for irrigation. However, these arguments did not sway the community, and the Cemetery Association accepted the cemetery in 1939.

The grave shown in the drawing dates from this period. It is the burial site of Minnie Starr Slater, who died in December, 1939. She was the wife of Charles Slater, who, along with Minnie, homesteaded across the river from Fairbanks. (Their homestead became Slaterville, and Charles named many of the streets after family members. Minnie Street is named after Charles' wife.)

The cemetery association donated the cemetery to the City of Fairbanks in 1957. Under city management the cemetery continued to inter people, however, the cemetery was not set up as a "perpetual care" facility, and the interment fees never covered the continued upkeep of the graves. In later years groundskeeping was a low priority for the city and the cemetery deteriorated.

There are approximately 4,000 graves at the cemetery. Some of the better-known personalities interred there include Alaska's last Territorial Governor, Mike Stepovich; Elam Harnish, the Klondike gold miner who was the inspiration for Jack London's book, *Burning Daylight*; and Fannie Quigley of Kantishna fame.

In 1994 annual volunteer cleanups began in order to improve the cemetery. The City, unable to keep the grounds adequately maintained, transferred the cemetery to Fairbanks Funeral Home (FFH) in 2007. One of the accomplishments of FFH was setting aside a portion of the cemetery for Native burials. The cemetery is now owned and operated by Birch Hill Cemetery, Inc., a non-profit corporation.

Over the years the Pioneers of Alaska has become involved with Birch Hill Cemetery. In 2003 the Pioneers' Igloo No. 4 Foundation began placing and replacing markers on the graves of pioneers around Interior Alaska. Erica Miller, a member of the Pioneer's Fairbanks chapter, told me that to date they have placed 149 markers at Birch Hill Cemetery, and another 121 at the Clay Street Cemetery in Fairbanks.

They have also placed markers at the Livengood, Manley, Circle Hot Springs, Deadwood (near Central), and the Nenana city cemeteries. Volunteers from across the state (including one from Nome) have also recently participated in a Pioneers of Alaska project to clean up the cemeteries at Chitina and McCarthy.

Cemeteries are often the only evidence left from early settlements, It is gratifying that some individuals and groups are working to keep these important historic sites alive.

Sources:

- "Birch Hill slope site favored," in *Fairbanks Daily News-Miner*. 12-10-1938
- Conversation with Doug Ketterer, caretaker for Birch Hill Cemetery. 2014
- Conversation with Erica Miller, member of Fairbanks Women's Igloo No. 8, Pioneers of Alaska. 2014
- Fairbanks North Star Borough property records
- "First Burial on Birch Hill," In *Alaska Miner*. 11-8-1938
- "Legion not yet for hill cemetery," In *Fairbanks Daily News-Miner*. 12-14-1938
- "Place to remember." Cynthia Rinear Bethune. In *Fairbanks Daily News-Miner*. 9-19-1999

Fairbanks - Farmers Loop

KFAR radio transmitter building on Farmers Loop road in 2014

## KFAR Radio – Cap Lathrop's gift to Interior Alaska

Within a few years of commercial radio's birth in the Lower 48, radio stations began popping up in Alaska. In 1922 the Northern Commercial Company (NC Co.) started KLAY radio station in Fairbanks. Unfortunately for Fairbanks residents, the radio station was short lived. When the NC Co. discovered that in order to keep its license it had to offer airtime on its "company" radio station to other Fairbanks businesses, it turned the transmitter off.

KFQD in Anchorage went on the air in 1924, Ketchikan's KGBU in 1926, and KINY in Juneau in 1935. It wasn't until Austin "Cap" Lathrop built KFAR in 1939, that radio, which became so vital to Northern life and culture, came back to Interior Alaska.

It was at the prodding of Miriam Dickey, Lathrop's executive secretary, that Cap decided to start a radio station. Lathrop was reportedly "the richest man in Alaska" and could have lived and spent his money anywhere in the United States. However, he wanted to reinvest his wealth in Alaska, and Dickey convinced him a radio station to serve the needs of Interior Alaska would be a fitting legacy.

The Fairbanks area at that time had a population of about 8,000 people. Augie Hiebert, one of the radio engineers instrumental in setting up the new station, related in his book, *Airwaves over Alaska*, that a 100-250 watt transmitter would have been appropriate for a town the size of Fairbanks.

However, Cap envisioned a radio station that could reach all of Interior Alaska, so he installed a 1,000 watt transmitter. In a promotional book published the first year of the station's operation, its coverage area was advertised as the Fairbanks vicinity; the railbelt north of Anchorage; the Circle, Kuskokwim, and Iditarod districts; the Seward Peninsula; and the region around Dawson City.

During commercial radio's infancy, radio stations could choose their own call letters, and Cap held a contest to select the new station's name. The winning entry was KFAR, which stood for "Key for Alaska Riches." The station's slogan became "From the Top of the Word to you." It began transmitting on Oct. 1, 1939.

KFAR's broadcasting studio was on the top floor of the newly completed four-story Lathrop Building on Second Avenue in Fairbanks, and a transmitter building (shown in the drawing) was constructed at mile 5 of the farm road (now Farmers Loop). The transmitter's 300-foot tower can be seen in the background. The building, constructed of reinforced concrete like Cap's other businesses in Fairbanks, was designed by Marcus Pritica, who also designed the Lacey Street Theater for Lathrop. As with the Lacey, the transmitter building is decidedly Art Deco in design.

The 27-foot by 72-foot building, which has 14-foot ceilings in most of the building, is divided into three sections. The middle section housed the stations transmitters and other equipment. To the right of the central section is the radio engineer's small one-bedroom apartment, and the other side contains a garage and storage area.

The transmitter facility is no longer in service and is currently used for storage by the Fairbanks Golf and Country Club, which has almost as long a history at KFAR. Cap entered into a gentleman's agreement with the club for a 99-year lease on the 60 acres around the transmitter, and the golf course opened on June 21, 1946.

Borealis Broadcasting Company bought the radio station in the 1980s, and in 1989 sold the Farmer's Loop property to the golf club. According to borough property records, the old transmitter building has settled considerably over the years, but is still in fairly good condition. Golf course manager, Matt Taylor, told me that some day the club would like to convert the building into its clubhouse.

Sources:

- *Airwaves over Alaska, the story of Pioneer Broadcaster, Augie Hiebert.* as told by his daughter, Robin Ann Chlupach. Sammamish Press. 1992
- *Alaska's First Homegrown Millionaire, Life and Times of Cap Lathrop.* Elizabeth Tower. 2006
- Conversation with Matt Taylor, Fairbanks Gold Club manager. 2104
- *KFAR Keybook of Interior Alaska.* Midnight Sun Broadcasting Company. 1939
- "King of clubs: 50 years of swinging times." Bob Eley. in *Fairbanks Daily News-Miner.* 6-16-1996

Fairbanks - University of Alaska, W. Tanana Drive

The barn and farm manager's house at the UAF Experiment Farm in 2013

## UAF Experiment Farm history reflects saga of Alaska agriculture

Pictured in the drawing are the two oldest buildings at the University of Alaska Experiment Farm: the manager's residence and the barn, both built in 1940. The farm was originally part of the Federal government's agricultural station project in Alaska, which was begun in 1897 in response to the gold rushes at the end of the 1800s, and the incumbent need to increase Alaska's agricultural industry.

Westerners in Alaska had been dabbling in agriculture since the Russian occupation in the 1700s and 1800s with little success beyond kitchen gardens. Under U.S. ownership little changed in Alaska, and the curious situation existed where one could file a mining claim, but no means existed to legally acquire land for agricultural purposes.

That started to change with the opening of the first agricultural station in Alaska at Sitka in 1897. The number of agricultural stations rapidly expanded during the next decade, with stations being started at Kodiak (1898), Kenai (1899), Rampart (1900) and Copper Center (1903).

The city of Fairbanks (established in 1902) had the benefit of being situated in an area of great agricultural potential (the head of Alaska's agricultural station program estimated that over 100,000 acres in the Tanana Valley could be developed), and the local Chamber of Commerce lobbied the federal government for its own station. In May, 1906, the U.S. government set aside 1,400 acres of land near the present site of the University of Alaska for a station.

In 1915 Congress approved funds and a land transfer to establish the Alaska Agricultural College and School of Mines next to the agricultural station at Fairbanks. Additional funds were appropriated by the Alaska Territorial Legislature several years later and the college opened in 1922.

All of the Fairbanks experiment station facilities were transferred from the federal government to the college in 1931. Much of the land that the university's West Ridge facilities now sit on was once experiment station fields. There were even a few fields on the far side of the ridge near Smith Lake.

In a 2006 *Fairbanks Daily News-Miner* article, Pat Holloway, professor of horticulture at the University of Alaska, said that the station was primarily meant to be a demonstration farm. But, as with the other stations, it also worked to develop crops and livestock suited to Alaska's conditions. Its work in developing crops for Interior Alaska and close proximity to Fairbanks allowed it to help the community in times of need.

The book, *Like a Tree to the Soil,* by Josephine Papp and Josie Phillips, relates that during the winter of 1915-16 there was a serious shortage of horse feed, and by spring, farmers had been forced to use their grain seed to feed livestock.

The Fairbanks station, which had been raising grain for five years, had 1100 bushels of wheat, rye, barley, oat and buckwheat seed stockpiled by the spring of 1916. From that stockpile it advanced seed to area farmers, on the condition that they repay in kind after the fall harvest. The loans were a lifesaver, and every farmer who received seed repaid their loan by January of 1917.

The station also worked with animal husbandry, raising its own horses, cattle and sheep. Not all of its experiments were successful though. Old photos in the UAF archives show yaks at the station. One of the photo captions states that they tried crossing yaks with Galloway cattle from Scotland to get an animal that could winter outside in Alaska. The experiment was disappointing, with "meat tough as \*\*\*\*!" Other photos show a similar disappointing experiment, crossing domestic sheep with wild mountain sheep.

The farm still provides research and demonstration projects in forest management, agronomy, animal science, horticulture, and resources management, and although recent budget cuts have impacted the farm's programs, Alan Tonne, the farm's manager, told me he was confident that it will survive.

Located on West Tanana Drive on the lower edge of the UAF campus, the farm has 260 acres of cropland and 50 acres of forest land used for demonstration projects and research. Farm facilities include two residences, a visitor center, barn, greenhouse, grain handling facility, small saw mill, feed mill, maintenance shop, and several storage facilities. The Georgeson Botanical Garden is located adjacent to the farm.

Sources:

- "100 years of Agricultural Research in Alaska," in *Agroborealis,* Vol. 3, No. 1, 1998
- "Alaska History of Agriculture," *National Preservation Program for Agricultural Literature*, from United States Agricultural Information Network. no date
- Conversation with Alan Tonne, experiment farm manager. 2013
- "Experimental farm celebrates a century." Robinson Duffy. in *Fairbanks Daily News-Miner*. 6-25-2006,
- *Like a Tree to the Soil, a history of farming in Alaska's Tanana Valley, 1903-1940*. Josephine Papp & Josie Phillips. School of Natural Sciences and Agricultural Sciences, University of Alaska Fairbanks. 2007

Fairbanks - University of Alaska, Tok Lane

Constitution Hall at the University of Alaska, Fairbanks in 2012

## Constitution Hall played important role in state's formation

Ernest Patty's tenure as president of the University of Alaska (from 1953-1960) was a time of building. According to Terrence Cole's book, *The Cornerstone on College Hill*, during those seven years the faculty almost doubled in size, the student body increased by 237 percent, and the value of the university's physical plant increased by 650 percent. New buildings were completed at the rate of one per year.

One of those new buildings was the student union building. Construction on this building, now called Constitution Hall, was begun in the summer of 1955 and completed that fall. Designed by the architectural firm of Foss, Malcom and Olson of Juneau, it was built by Pacific Construction Company of Fairbanks.

The reinforced concrete building, as designed and built, has two stories plus a full basement, and two extensions. An L-shaped single-story extension wraps around the building's south and southwest corner and a single-story rectangular extension with basement is located in at the rear.

The construction of the student union coincided with a singular event in Alaska history—the Alaska Constitutional Convention held during the winter of 1955-56.

In 1955 Alaska was still a territory, but momentum had been building for several years to draft a state constitution, in the hopes that it would spur Congress to approve statehood for Alaska.

The Alaska legislature passed a bill in March 1955 authorizing a constitutional convention. Although there was ample room in Juneau to hold the meetings, the University of Alaska was chosen as a neutral site away from the partisan atmosphere of the territorial capital. Convention organizers and campus administrators decided that the new student union, with meeting rooms, food service and even a beauty parlor, would be an ideal meeting venue.

Fifty-five delegates from across the territory arrived in Fairbanks for the November 8th opening ceremony. Workmen were still putting the finishing touches on the building even as the convention convened. The opening ceremonies were actually held in the school gymnasium in order to accommodate all the delegates, dignitaries and spectators.

The next day delegates moved to the student union. The regents officially named the building "Constitution Hall" at their November 30th annual meeting. (According to a November 8, 1955, issue of the *Fairbanks Daily News-Miner*, the gym actually bore that name first, temporarily holding the title for the first day's opening ceremonies.)

The choice of the University of Alaska as the convention's location proved to be a wise one, and the meetings were relatively free from partizan politics. KFAR radio broadcast many of the meetings. (The Alaska State Archives has digitized about 220 hours of these recordings.)

Delegates worked until early February on the draft document, signing it on Feb. 6. (It was signed in the gym, to accommodate the estimated 1,000 people who attended).

Alaska's new constitution was approved by Alaska voters in April 1955. It did not become law until three years later when Congress passed a statehood bill in June 1958. Alaska was admitted as the 49th state in the union in January 1959.

When the constitutional convention ended, Constitution Hall reverted to its originally designed function as a student union. It housed a bookstore; recreation room; beauty shop; student lounge; offices for student government, student publications, and alumni association; and faculty lounge. When Alaska's first public radio station, KUAC-FM, began broadcasting in 1962, the university made room for its offices in Constitution Hall.

The building remained the student union until Wood Center opened in 1972. Constitution Hall is now home to the UAF bookstore, campus post office, barbershop, alumni association office, KSUA-FM (the student-run radio station), and United Campus Ministry.

While the interior has seen some major remodeling, the exterior has changed little since 1955. The front entrance has been modernized, but all the wood window frames and sashes are original. The building still evokes much the same atmosphere as when it was constructed. It was added to the National Register of Historic Places in 2005.

Sources:

- "Constitution Hall." Valerie Robancho-Andresen. From *UA Journey*. 2011
- "Constitution Hall – National Register of Historic Places Nomination Form." Terrence Cole. National Park Service. 2005
- *Fairbanks Daily News-Miner articles.* November 8th & 9th, 1955
- "Governing Alaska, The Constitutional Convention." Alaska History and Cultural Studies website. 2004-2015
- *The Cornerstone on College Hill*. Terrence Cole. University of Alaska Press. 1994
- *49 at last! The battle for Alaska Statehood*. Clause-M. Naske. Alaska Northwest Publishing. 1973

The Bunnell House in about 2000

## Bunnell House still an important part of University

The Alaska College of Agriculture and School of Mines (now the University of Alaska Fairbanks) got off to a slow and shaky start. Established in 1917 with an initial appropriation of $60,000 from the territorial legislature, the school's trustees immediately began construction of a classroom building on what quickly became known as "College Hill."

The legislature met biannually, and by the time it next convened in 1919, the classroom building was essentially complete. However, the college had negligible funds left to equip the building, hire instructors, and open the school.

Although $50,000 was requested, no bills were passed that year to fund the college, so its trustees were forced to wait another two years, hoping the next legislature would be more amenable. In 1921, the college did receive $41,000 to finish and equip the classroom building, hire a faculty and build a residence for the school's president (shown in the drawing). An amendment to the funding bill stipulated the cost for the president's house was not to exceed $8,000.

Almost all the college's early buildings, being of wood-frame construction, were eventually replaced. However, the president's residence, known now as the Bunnell House (in honor of the college's first president, Charles E. Bunnell), still survives, and is the oldest campus building still in use.

The president's residence was a six-room wood-frame cottage with full basement. Constructed in the summer of 1922 (the college began classes that fall), the house was located adjacent to the only road onto campus, about where the Lola Tilly Commons is now located.

A fire gutted the building in 1931, but the university immediately rebuilt. The cause of the fire was never discovered, although arson was suspected.

Finances were tight during the college's early years. Everyone, from President Bunnell down to the students, worked multiple jobs.

Twelve students enrolled during the college's first year, and except for one senior, all were freshman. This meant no advanced courses for most of the instructors. According to William Cashen's book, *Farthest North College President*, Earl Pilgrim, the metallurgy instructor, spent many of his free hours that first semester painting and wallpapering the interior of the president's residence.

Bunnell was a tireless and dedicated worker. Neil Davis, in his book, *The College Hill Chronicles*, writes, "Most of President Bunnell's waking hours were spent in his office or working somewhere else on the campus. Late at night he retired to his small frame residence, which stood like a guard house near the entrance to the campus and allowed him to observe all who entered there and at what hour."

President Bunnell lived in that house until his death in 1956. This was in spite of the fact that he resigned as college president in 1949. Terris Moore was appointed the new president that same year and Bunnell was given the title of "President Emeritus."

At the regents meeting in spring 1949 (by this time the college had become the University of Alaska), Bunnell informed the regents that he had no intention of leaving the president's residence, and Moore and the regents decided not to force the issue. Moore and his family were housed temporarily in the university infirmary until moving into newly built quarters later that year.

Two years after Bunnell's death the building was relocated to its present location on Chatanika Drive, behind the university fire station. Until the 1970s it was utilized by the Home Economics Department, and also saw service as faculty housing. The building now houses the university's Early Childhood Development program.

Situated on a hillside, the Bunnell house still has a lovely view of Chena and Tanana River lowlands (albeit facing a different direction). It is also still used for education, something Charles Bunnell would be pleased with.

Sources:

- *Farthest North College President, Charles E. Bunnell and the early history of the University of Alaska*. William R. Cashen. University of Alaska Press. 1972
- "History of the Presidents' Residence - Part I." from *UA Journey*. 2015
- "If these walls could talk, the Bunnell House." Scott McCrea. University of Alaska Fairbanks, Marketing and Publications. August 2006
- *The Cornerstone on College Hill*. Terrence Cole. University of Alaska Press. 1994
- *The College Hill Chronicles, How the University of Alaska Came of Age*. Neil Davis. University of Alaska Foundation. 1992

Fairbanks - Chena Pump Road

Pump House Restaurant in the fall of 2013

# Fairbanks Exploration Company's pump house a watering hole of a different sort

The Pump House Restaurant is one of the premiere dining establishments in the Fairbanks area. However, more than 80 years ago it began its life as a different sort of watering hole.

It began as a pumping station to provide water for the Fairbanks Exploration Company's (F.E. Co.) dredging operations in the Cripple Creek area on the opposite side of Chena Ridge.

The F.E. Co. began dredging north of Fairbanks in the late 1920s, with its first dredges located on Goldstream and Cleary creeks. Water for dredges north of the city came from the Davidson Ditch, which brought water to Fairbanks from the Chatanika River.

When the company decided to dredge near Ester, it needed another water source. The volume of water from creeks in the area was insufficient to provide the volume of high pressure water necessary to hydraulically strip away thick overburden above the gold-bearing gravels and to thaw frozen gravels. Consequently, the F.E. Co. decided to pump water from the Chena River over Chena Ridge.

National Register of Historic Places documents state that from 1931 to 1933 the F.E. Co. constructed a pump house, three 26-inch pipelines from the river to the top of Chena Ridge, and three miles of open ditches beyond the ridge to carry water to the diggings.

The original pump house building was 20-feet wide by 108-feet long, with an 8-foot deep by 20-foot wide bay protuding from its south side. It had a gable roof with five skylights to provide interior illumination. Both the roof and exterior walls were covered with corrugated metal sheathing.

The pump house was set back about 100 feet from the river, with a raceway on the north side of the building carrying water from the river. (The water intake apparatus can be seen in the drawing foreground.) Ten 14-inch double-suction centrifugal pumps (rated at 6,000 gpm) pumped the water up Chena Ridge. Each pump had a 400-hp motor, and electricity was provided by the F.E. Company power plant on Illinois Street.

For those of you wondering where all that water ended up, eventually it flowed back into the Chena River. According to John Boswell's history of the F.E. Company, two options were considered for routing the return water. The first was a 10,200-foot tunnel through Chena Ridge. The second was a six-mile-long open ditch.

The company finally decided the open ditch was more practical. However, even it was not without engineering difficulties since keeping the ditch at the proper grade meant excavating 100-foot-deep cuts in places. The remains of this ditch can still be seen.

After the F.E. Co. shut down its Cripple Creek operations in the 1960s, it closed the pump house. The building sat derelict for years, surrounded by pieces of mining equipment and encroaching trees.

In 1976, Bill and Vivian Bubbel bought the property, planning to convert the building into a restaurant. By 1978 they had completed initial renovations for the Pump House Restaurant.

The Bubbels wanted the building to retain its historical significance so renovations incorporated as much of the original structure as possible. The building's north exterior looks much the same as it did when it was used as a pump house, with the exterior metal wall sheathing being original. A new main entrance on the north side of the building was added, and kitchen and service additions were constructed on the south side of the building.

Inside, the main dining room space has been kept open, and patrons can still see the underside of the original metal roofing. A new insulated roof was installed over the top of that.

The Bubbles, who still own the restaurant, had made additional improvements, including adding a large deck between the restaurant and river. The building was placed on the National Register of Historic Places in 1980, and the Bubbles intend to maintain the building's historical authenticity.

Sources:

- Conversation with Bill Bubbel, co-owner of the Pump House Restaurant. 2014
- *Historic Resources in the Fairbanks North Star Borough*. Janet Mattheson & Bruce Haldeman. Fairbanks North Star Borough, 1981
- *History of Alaskan Operations of United States Smelting, Refining and Mining Company*. John C. Boswell. Mineral Industries research Laboratory, University of Alaska. 1979
- "Chena Pump House - National Register of Historic Places Inventory-Nomination Form." Jane Galblum. National Park Service, 1980

# The River of Ink

by Howard Haynes, In February 1948 issue of *Alaska Life*,
*the Territorial Magazine*

*For yarns all wool and two yards wide. old Yukon Bill won fame;*
*One day he told about Ink Creek, and how it got it's name.*

*He'd set his traps for 'rats and mink in frozen Wild Goose Slough,*
*And had wood cut to heat his shack when icy blizzards blew.*

*Though pitch-pine chunks were fine for heat, Bill's stove soon failed to draw;*
*His bean-pot froze so hard it took three days for it to thaw.*

*The nerve strain cracked Bill's peace and calm, with temper over-ripe.*
*Bill burned his pair of rubber boots to clean the clogged stove pipe.*

*And then the black soot fogged in the sky high over Bear Snout Peak,*
*Until spring rains washed it down into the nearby creek.*

*Bill wrote a note to prove his yarn was no wild-eyed pipe-dream,*
*And scrawled the words with pen dipped in that tumbling soot-black stream!*

www.ingramcontent.com/pod-product-compliance
Lightning Source LLC
Chambersburg PA
CBHW082042200426
43209CB00053B/1340